The United States and Latin America

The United States and Latin America

By RICHARD J. WALTON

★ ★ ★ ★ ★

A Clarion Book
THE SEABURY PRESS, New York

ACKNOWLEDGMENTS

Grateful acknowledgment is made to the following book publishers and authors for permission to use copyrighted material from the titles listed:

Aguilar, Alonzo, *Pan-Americanism from Monroe to the Present: A View from the Other Side*. New York: Monthly Review Press, 1968. Copyright © 1968 by Monthly Review Press. Reprinted by permission of Monthly Review Press.

Barnet, Richard J., *Intervention and Revolution*. New York: World Publishing Co., 1968.

Bemis, Samuel F., *The Latin American Policy of the United States*. New York: Harcourt Brace Jovanovich, Inc., 1943.

DeVoto, Bernard, *The Year of Decision: 1846*. Boston: Houghton Mifflin Company, 1961, p. 13. Reprinted by permission of Houghton Mifflin Company.

Morgan, H. Wayne, *America's Road to Empire: The War with Spain and Overseas Expansion*. New York: John Wiley and Sons, Inc., 1965. Copyright © 1965 by H. Wayne Morgan. Reprinted by permission of John Wiley and Sons, Inc.

Munro, Dana G., *Intervention and Dollar Diplomacy in the Caribbean 1900–1921*. Princeton, N.J.: Princeton University Press, 1964. Copyright © 1964 by Princeton University Press.

Pendle, George, *A History of Latin America*. London: Penguin Books, Ltd. Copyright © 1963 by George Pendle.

Tannenbaum, Frank H., "Political Dilemma in Latin America." *Foreign Affairs*, April, 1960. Copyright held by the Council on Foreign Relations, Inc., New York, N.Y.

Second Printing

Copyright © 1972 by Richard J. Walton
ISBN: 0-8164-3074-8
Library of Congress Catalog Card Number: 76-171860

Printed in the United States of America

FOR GARY

Foreword

This book can be only an introduction to a subject as vast as the hemisphere it attempts to encompass. Each of the score of nations of Latin America has had a long and often complicated relationship with the United States, and each has a rich and colorful history meriting an entire book unto itself. Yet though oversimplifications will necessarily result, there is a validity for attempting to deal with the relations between the United States and Latin America as a whole. For despite real and frequent differences in the relations between the United States and various individual Latin nations, there has been since the beginning a United States attitude toward Latin America. Conversely, there has been a fairly consistent Latin American attitude toward the United States based on the region's common heritage, tradition, and history. It is this relationship that this book will attempt to trace from the uncertain beginning to the uncertain present, with an even more uncertain look into the future.

Perhaps it would be useful first to define some geographic

terms. *Latin America* is the most inclusive, covering all of the Western Hemisphere south of the United States border, including the Caribbean islands. *Central America* is that narrower strip of land (including part of Mexico) which connects *North America* and *South America*.

Of the Caribbean islands, I have excluded Puerto Rico for the purposes of this book, which deals entirely with the international relations between the United States and its southern neighbors. Although Puerto Rico is Latin American in culture, history, and tradition, it has been a U.S. possession since the Spanish-American War, gradually evolving from a colony to a commonwealth with internal self-government. Its people are American citizens, free to move to the United States and possessing full voting rights.

One other thing also must be said before we start. Since it was Central and South America that first made lasting impact on world history, they have perhaps a stronger claim to the word "American." But throughout this book, except where the context makes the broader meaning obvious, I will use the word in its various forms to mean the United States and its people. The reason is one of practicality. There are such words as Latin American, Brazilian, Mexican, etc., for the peoples of those areas, but there is no such word, other than American, for the people of the United States. Although the term *norteamericano* springs naturally to the lips of a Latin American, its English translation does not come easily to an American. So, if apologies are due, I cheerfully offer them.

Contents

The history of U.S. relations with Cuba—and with other Latin American republics too—is a story, on the U.S. side, of good intentions and self-righteousness, idealism and self-interest, jingoism and exuberant commercialism; and on the other side of inexperience, poverty, and corruption, the desire to have U.S. aid and the fear of U.S. domination.

George Pendle
A History of Latin America

1
The Beginning

In a sense it all began on October 12, 1492 when Christopher Columbus, as all the world knows, stepped ashore on a wooded, fertile island, proclaimed it San Salvador, took possession of it for the king and queen of Spain and said a prayer. At that moment Columbus established two elements that are of paramount importance in Latin America to this day: the Spanish heritage and the Roman Catholic Church.

But the story really began centuries before in the dreams of European man of an earthly paradise far to the west across the ocean sea—dreams of a beautiful land, fertile and rich in all the bounties of nature, rich most of all in that soft and malleable metal of so little real value to man but so prized by him: gold. This El Dorado of dream and myth and romantic hope captured the Europeans' imagination and for once the reality equaled the dream, perhaps even surpassed it.

The presence of vast quantities of gold in Latin America led the Europeans, in their greed, to impose an economy of plunder and exploitation rather than of development. Latin Amer-

I

ica might have been richer had it been poorer, had its Spanish
and Portuguese conquerors been forced to develop its entire
range of natural resources instead of enriching their monarchs
with gold and gold and more gold.

Although John Cabot rediscovered Newfoundland (it had
been discovered first by the Norsemen) and claimed it for the
English Crown only five years after Columbus discovered Central America, North America lagged a century behind its
southern counterpart in settlement. The cold cruel winters, the
stormy North Atlantic, contributed to this lag but so, no
doubt, did the failure of the early English and French and
Portuguese explorers to find gold in North America. They
were disappointed, to be sure, but when the settlers did begin
to come to North America in the early 1600s, they found other
riches than gold, not so alluring nor so glamorous nor so easy
to exploit, but of far greater real value. There were fertile soil
and endless forests that provided wood for building houses and
ships. The earth of North America was rich with useful minerals, iron and coal, and in the fields and forests there were ani-
mals for food and furs. Off the coasts swam fish in abundance.

But even now in the 1970s gold, a metal useful for little else
but ornamentation and hoarding, has the power to influence
the economies of the richest nations. (Witness the "dollar crisis" of recent years, caused by the fact that the United States
does not own enough gold to redeem dollars held in other
countries and theoretically redeemable in gold.) So who can
blame the Spanish and Portuguese for their excitement when
Columbus reported that the Indians of Latin America—so-
called because he thought he had discovered the long-sought
ocean passage to Asia—"wore little pieces of gold in their per-
forated noses" and told tales of a king "who owned many ves-

sels filled with gold"? [1] Remember how Americans flocked to
California in 1849 when gold was discovered at Sutter's Mill!

Although Columbus himself never found much gold, he did
establish the first permanent Spanish settlement in the New
World, on Hispaniola, the island now divided into the Dominican Republic and Haiti. And in his three return voyages he
discovered Central America and the northern shores of South
America, recognizing by the huge volume of water flowing
from the mouth of the Orinoco River (in present-day Venezuela) that he had reached a mighty continent, presumably
Asia. But the tales of gold were enough to spur other explorers
and they, too, heard stories of fabulous cities of gold.

Among the voyagers in those first years after Columbus'
journeys was a rich and scholarly Italian, Amerigo Vespucci,
who, although no sailor, journeyed across the ocean out of cu-
riosity. Believing that the discovery was not Asia but a new
continent, he called it the New World. And because his accounts of his travels were circulated through Europe before the
journals of Columbus were published, a German cartographer
in 1507 issued a map labeling the New World "America."
While a discredited Columbus died in 1506, the New World
he had discovered was given the name of a mere passenger on
one of the many ships that had followed in his wake. But although history never completely righted this wrong—America
these continents have remained—Columbus for centuries past
has been celebrated as the most famous explorer in the history
of the Western world. Voyagers to the moon have not dis-
placed him nor, most likely, will those who journey far into
space, for no one explorer has so profoundly changed the
course of human history.

In 1493, when Columbus first reported his discoveries to an

exultant Ferdinand and Isabella, they rushed to establish Spanish ownership of what they thought were islands off the coast of Asia. The Turks had barred the Mediterranean to Spanish merchant fleets and the Portuguese controlled the African coast. There had been no way for Spanish merchants to get from the Orient the spices vital for meat in those days long before refrigeration. Now at last their way to the Orient was clear.

The Spanish monarchs were aware, however, that the Portuguese king had similar ambitions. They approached the Pope who was recognized in the Christian kingdoms as having the authority to allocate new lands. It was a good time for the Spanish approach, for the Pope, Alexander VI, was a Spaniard who owed his office to the Spanish Crown. In May 1493 he issued a Papal Bull that divided the uncharted world between Spain and Portugal. It was a grand gesture by the Pope. He drew a line from pole to pole 100 leagues (300 miles) to the west of the Cape Verde Islands, Portuguese possessions about 400 miles west of the westernmost point of Africa. All to the west of this line would belong to Spain, all to the east to Portugal. Although the full dimensions of South America were not yet known, the Portuguese, superb navigators, could make a pretty shrewd guess that all of the New World would be to the west of the line; thus, they would get nothing.

Portugal refused to accept this demarcation, and after some bargaining the Spanish monarchs and the Portuguese king agreed in 1494 on the Treaty of Tordesillas, which set the line at 370 leagues (1,110 miles) west of the Cape Verde Islands. This, purely by chance, put much of what became Brazil within the Portuguese sphere. However, while this arrangement might have suited the Spanish and Portuguese rulers, it did not set well with the English and Dutch, who also had imperial aspirations and seagoing power to match. This, later reinforced by the religious tensions of the Reformation, caused the protracted wars on land and sea that finally shattered Spanish power.

But that was for the more distant future. In the immediate future other navigators flying the Spanish flag followed Columbus to what they, too, thought were Indian isles. Gradually it dawned on them that Vespucci was right, that a vast new continent stood between them and the Indies. They would have to find a way through or around. This became certain when Balboa and a few brave companions crossed the Isthmus of Panama to the Pacific in 1513, and when in 1521 the Portuguese navigator Magellan, sailing under the Spanish flag, beat his way through the straits at the southern tip of the continent that now bear his name. The tales of fabulous golden cities multiplied, however, and Spain decided that the New World was not an obstacle but the fabled El Dorado itself.

The period of pure exploration was over by about 1521. After that the explorers were also conquerors, *conquistadores.* They were extraordinary men, these conquistadores: Cortes, Pizarro, Valdiva, and the others. They were brutal and cruel, to be sure, but bold and brave and resourceful as well. They struck inland from the coasts of Latin America, knowing not where they were going, following those tales of golden cities. Pitifully few in number, they marched off into jungles and across mountain ranges. They were outnumbered always but they had horses and firearms which terrorized the Indians, who had never seen either. All that saved them was their courage, toughness, and ingenuity.

Even if one's sympathies are with the invaded and not the

invaders, one must recognize the latter's military achievements. Within a few decades after Columbus set foot on San Salvador, and well before permanent European settlements were established in North America, the conquistadores had overcome incredible odds and founded the cities that are still the great cities of Latin America. The Spaniards began to build Mexico City in 1521 on the ruins of the former Aztec capital (which they had destroyed). Quito (Ecuador) was founded in 1534 and Lima (Peru) in 1535. Buenos Aires was begun in 1536, only to be abandoned because of Indian attacks. But it was later reoccupied on its present site. The conquerors had founded Asuncion (Paraguay) a thousand miles up the Paraná River in 1537, and a year later Bogotá (Colombia) was founded. Santiago de Chile was founded in 1541 and even in the remote Andean fastnesses of Bolivia, Sucre was founded in 1538 and La Paz in 1548.

The conquerors were adventurers who sought gold and fame. They carried with them also a fanatical desire to convert the infidel Indians to Christianity, relying more on the sword than the cross as their instrument of conversion. Missionaries invariably accompanied them, blessing the new cities and supervising the construction of a church, always one of the first buildings. Thus, Spanish cities, Catholic cities, sprang up all over the continent save in that vast area reserved to Portugal by the Papal Bull. Both influences are strong to this day.

Unfortunately space does not permit a more detailed account of the Spanish conquests, for they are stories of incomparable adventure. But they have been well told elsewhere.[2] We must, however, take a brief look at what the conquistadores found, for a knowledge of the land and peoples is essential. To neither have come the changes that were experienced in the

United States. Large areas of Latin America are still undeveloped and the population, although the Spaniards and the Portuguese have ruled for centuries, is still largely Indian. In the United States the Indians are numerically insignificant, having been killed or driven off their land into reservations which, most often, only offered poverty and degradation.

First the land itself. There is a vast difference between North America, particularly the United States, and Latin America. While most of the United States is in the temperate zones of highest human productivity, most of Latin America is in the tropics, the area of lowest human productivity. This is very important. Only in the temperate regions of the narrowest section of Central America, in parts of Chile and Argentina, in the tropical highlands, and in scattered other areas of Latin America has the climate been as favorable for human life and activity as in the United States.

Geography has also conspired against Latin America in other ways. The formidable mountain ranges, the dense, hot jungles, and the wide rivers have contributed to its fragmentation. Further, the rains, generally speaking, have fallen in North America where they are most useful and in Latin America where (the tropical jungles) they are least useful. This explains in large part why European settlers populated all of the United States and the habitable southern regions of Canada, whereas a European population predominates only in relatively small areas of Latin America—southern Brazil, Argentina, Cuba, Uruguay, and Costa Rica. In most of the rest of Latin America the population is predominantly native Indian and mixed racial strains or, where slaves were introduced from Africa, black and racially mixed.

While the question of race and culture is a difficult and

complex one, it can be said that the Europeans brought with them cultures economically more developed. But here there is another crucial difference between North America and Latin America. In North America the English and French and Dutch settlers came to work themselves, often at hard physical labor, to develop the land. The predominate tendency in Latin America was for the Europeans to use slave Indian or African labor to exploit the land, shipping its wealth back to the mother countries. Over a period of centuries this changed with the planting of sugar cane in Cuba, the cultivation of rubber in Brazil, coffee in several countries, cattle in Argentina, and mining in Chile, Peru, and Bolivia. But in the critical early decades the Spaniards and Portuguese practiced an economy of exploitation, not development.

To say that the Europeans brought a more modern, economically advanced culture is not to imply that the Indians lacked highly developed cultures of their own. Quite the contrary. The conquistadores often marveled at what they found. One of Cortes' men wrote upon his first sight of Tenochtitlán, the ancient Aztec capital of Emperor Montezuma in Mexico, "Never yet did man see, hear, or dream of anything equal to the spectacle which appeared before our eyes." [3] Cortes himself called it "the most beautiful city in the world," an island city of stone ramparts and palaces, with precious gems set in pillars of solid gold. To the Aztecs gold meant beauty; to the Spaniards it meant riches. Soon the Aztec wealth was looted and the once proud people reduced to peonage.

In Peru, Francisco Pizarro encountered the Incas, whose stone roads and buildings were erected with a skill that has caused many of them to endure to this day, though to this day their engineering methods remain a mystery. King Atahualpa ruled over a vast, rich, and well-organized state in the Andean highlands. There was gold and silver in abundance and the people were skilled in crafts. Pizarro, who had returned to Spain to report to Charles V on the great wealth of the Incas, was named Governor and Captain-General of Peru. He raised a force and after a two-year march from the coast of Ecuador reached the fertile high valley of Cajamarca, where Atahualpa reigned. Pizarro invited Atahualpa to call on him. It was a treacherous invitation.

The Inca king came borne on a golden throne attended by hundreds of courtiers. He sat on his splendid throne and listened, no doubt puzzled, to a lively discourse by a Catholic priest on the authority of the Pope and the supremacy of the king of Spain. Then suddenly, on Pizarro's signal, the Spaniards fell upon their guests with swords and firearms, killing hundreds. Atahualpa was captured, treated like the prince he was, and allowed to be visited by the women of his court. He was even taught to play chess. Soon, he recognized that his captors had a passion for gold and he offered to have a large room filled with golden objects if Pizarro would set him free. The conquistador agreed, and every day for two months Indians filed in from all across the country to fill the room with golden vessels and ornaments.

Early in 1533 Pizarro received reinforcements and decided to push farther into the Inca Empire, to the fabled city of Cuzco. He ordered the Indian goldsmiths to melt their precious objects into gold bars. The required fifth was despatched to the Spanish Crown and the rest divided among the invaders according to rank. Pizarro took one more precaution before he moved on. He accused Atahualpa of treason and had him strangled to death. The Spaniards entered Cuzco unopposed in November and quickly stripped the city of its gold, the Spanish soldiers gambling it away in riotous nights of gaming. Pizarro decided that Cuzco was too remote a location from which to rule the vast empire he had conquered, so he founded Lima, the "City of Kings," on the coast. From there he explored and settled areas extending from Ecuador into Chile.

The Spanish conquerors encountered another great civilization, that of the Mayans in what is now Guatemala, Honduras, and much of neighboring Mexico. It flourished from about the fourth century A.D. until the arrival of the Spanish, although it may well have existed for centuries earlier. It was the richest of the pre-Colombian civilizations. Based on the cultivation of corn, it produced architecture, sculpture, painting, hieroglyphic writing, mathematics, astronomy, and chronology. The Mayans left, now largely hidden by jungle, magnificent temples, palaces and pyramids and upright slabs (stelae) covered with sculptured hieroglyphics.

Scientists have determined that the Mayans were the first in human history to understand the mathematical concept of zero. Their astronomy may have been more advanced than that of the Egyptians of the same period, and their calendar was more accurate in the sixth or seventh century than the Gregorian calendar nearly a thousand years later. Scholars have learned much about the Mayan civilization but they would have learned much more had the conquistadores, in a vain attempt to stamp out the Mayan religion, not destroyed many ancient records. But the Mayans, although their history shows there was little war among the city-states, resisted the Spanish long after the other Indian nations had submitted. They frequently defeated Spanish forces and one stronghold held out until nearly 1700. It is one of history's great misfortunes that the plundering Spaniards finally stamped out this magnificent civilization.

The treatment of the native Indians is a crucial distinction between the European (mainly British) settlers of North America and the Spanish settlers to the south. In the North the Europeans, whose economy was based on agriculture, found the Indians a nuisance and did whatever they could to get rid of them. In the South the Spaniards, although they were cruel in the extreme, came to realize that, all moral considerations aside, it was folly to kill the Indians. They were necessary to mine the precious metals in the mountains and to transport them to the sea. And since few of the conquerors brought their families with them, the Indian women were needed as wives. From these unions came the mestizos, who make up most of the population in all but a few of the Latin American nations today. Along the coasts and on the Caribbean islands, African slaves were imported when the Indians succumbed to European diseases for which they had no immunity and to the fearful labor in harsh tropical climates.

There were other differences between the settlements in North and Latin America. The settlers in the North came predominantly from Britain, where the historic movement was toward unification, whereas the Spaniards came from a land with a long tradition of separatism, one that continues to this day. (See the recent trials of the Basque nationalists.) While it was natural for the British colonies to come together, it was natural for the Spanish Crown to rule over separate viceroyalties and captaincies-general just as it ruled over separate regions of Spain—Castilla, Catalonia, Aragon, etc. Thus despite the great unifying influence of the Spanish court and the Roman Catholic Church, geographic and historic barriers caused the various Latin American countries to develop separately, although there have always been movements to unite neighboring countries or even, to a greater or lesser degree, the whole of Latin America.

Another great difference was founded in the Spaniard's traditional admiration for the charismatic leader, the "man on horseback," the *caudillo.* This predilection toward *personalismo* was strengthened by the history of Spain's first decades in the New World, when its leaders were swaggering soldiers of fortune. The tendency to put men above institutions has persisted all through Latin American history to this day. Indeed, its history is a succession of heroic (and sometimes infamous) names: Cortes, Pizarro, Bolívar, San Martín, Martí, Perón, Trujillo, Batista, Castro. The list is almost endless.

Related to this is perhaps the most telling difference of all. The British colonists in what came to be the United States and Canada were the products of a democratic, parliamentary tradition in which both at home and in the colonies the historic direction was toward greater self-rule. In Spanish and Portuguese America the tradition was of absolute rule by the Crown, carried out by viceroys who allowed very little self-government, even of local matters, in the colonies. From the earliest days until the successful revolutions in the early nineteenth century, authority in Spanish America resided entirely in the Crown.

Because of distance and poor communications, the Spanish kings could not always control their viceroys and captains-general. However, the colonists seldom grumbled against the king but about his incompetent or corrupt representatives. And while it is true that many Latin American revolutionary leaders believed fervently in the principles of democracy, when full independence was finally gained by their countries, there was absolutely no tradition, experience, or institutions of democracy for the new leaders to fall back on.

2
Spain's Grip Weakens

For several centuries after 1492 there was little intercourse between North and Latin America. Both England and Spain were jealous of their colonies and kept others away. However, the dynastic and religious wars of Europe had their influence. France lost to England all but a couple of small islands of its once vast holdings in what was to become Canada. Both Britain and France grabbed several islands in the Caribbean, and Britain for a time occupied Cuba. The Spanish galleons laden with gold became irresistible targets for freebooters and the Spanish Main with its pirates provided a vivid chapter in history. Spanish power crept farther into North America, establishing footholds in Florida and far up the Mississippi, and gaining control over vast areas in Texas, New Mexico, Arizona, and as far up the California coast as San Francisco. But Spain's grip on the far northern reaches of its Mexican Empire was never very strong.

Even after the thirteen American colonies had won their independence, the fledgling United States they formed was still

14

weak and could do little or nothing about English adventures in the upper Midwest and Spanish holdings in Florida and the Southwest. But Europe's inability to keep at peace worked to the young nation's benefit. The French Revolution and the subsequent Napoleonic wars sapped the strength of Spain and Portugal. In 1800 Spain had to give up the immense Louisiana territory to France. If the fortunes of war had given this land to England, the entire course of U.S. history would have been changed. For then Britain, which by no means had lost its desire for a North American empire, would have encircled the infant nation from the mouth of the Mississippi to the St. Lawrence River.

Even in the hands of the ambitious and powerful Napoleon, the Louisiana territory was a threat to the United States for he, too, wanted to reestablish his nation's North American empire. Again the fortunes of European war benefited the United States. Facing renewed conflict with Britain, Napoleon decided to raise money by selling the enormous Louisiana territory. President Thomas Jefferson snapped it up in 1803, thus doubling American territory and opening the West to settlement.

Then when Napoleon conquered Spain, its colonies in the New World, except for Cuba, began a series of rebellions. Part of it was a desire for freedom sparked by the American Revolution and fanned by the French Revolution. But part of it was the desire of the Spanish colonists to have all the fruits of the New World for themselves. The United States was sympathetic to the rebellions. It knew virtually nothing of Spanish America but it was instinctively sympathetic to American peoples seeking their independence from European rulers.

During the periods of English–Spanish wars some American

ships had traded in the Caribbean and a few American consulates had been established. This practice was expanded during the period, beginning about 1808, when the Latin American rebellions began to break out, particularly when the rebels sent envoys to the United States to seek help. The major move in this direction came in 1808, when the Prince Regent of Portugal, fleeing Napoleon, transferred his court to Rio de Janeiro. Jefferson sent a cordial message by the hand of a consul who was formally received by the Prince Regent. But Jefferson was unsuccessful in competing with Britain for commercial favor in Brazil. Indeed, as Spanish strength weakened in Latin America, Britain, with its superior economic strength and great naval and merchant fleets, soon became the dominant European power.

With Spanish power in the New World crumbling, it is understandable that the United States was eager to take Florida. Not only was it a natural accession but Britain clearly had its eyes on it. Since there were not enough Spanish settlers in Florida—most of the settlers were Americans with Spanish grants—for it to become an independent nation, there was no real obstacle to American annexation. The question was how to go about it.

As Spanish authority in Florida continued to collapse, President James Madison in 1810 simply seized West Florida and attached it to Louisiana. Then on January 15, 1811 the Senate and the House in a joint resolution declared that "the United States . . . cannot without serious inquietude see any part" of the territory adjoining the southern border of the United States "pass into the hand of any foreign power." The resolution also provided for the temporary occupation of that territory, although it shall "remain subject to a future negotiation." The meaning was clear: Britain, keep your hands off.

The War of 1812 complicated things. The United States suffered immediate reverses and, with things going badly, was as eager to avoid getting involved with Spain as Spain was eager to avoid conflict with the United States. Thus the rebellions to the south were deprived of continuing American assistance and the United States was spared having another enemy. Because Britain was preoccupied with its historic European struggle with Napoleon, the United States luckily escaped the War of 1812 with its territory intact.

When Napoleon was defeated in 1814, the United States was not eager to take on Spain and its English ally, so it reestablished diplomatic relations with Spain and embarked on a course of neutrality between Spain and its rebellious colonies. The government of the United States may have decided to be neutral but its people were openly pro-rebellion and did not even attempt to hide violations of the neutrality acts. Americans sold weapons and ships and even manned privateers that raided Spanish shipping. And when the United States did bring violators to trial, it could never find a jury to issue convictions. The Spanish minister to Washington denounced these violations bitterly but he soon came to realize that nothing could be done.

Even this empty neutrality was precarious. Spain stalled on talks on Florida that would preserve the formal neutrality. The United States, for its part, threatened to occupy the rest of Florida or recognize the rebels, or do both, if Spain did not settle the Florida question. Britain stood in the wings. Conservative Britain did not want the United States to recognize the rebellious colonies but it was not prepared to help Spain put down the revolts. It hoped for independent monarchies which might help head off the historic movement toward the hated republican form of government. But the despotic Ferdinand VII of Spain refused British mediation; he was still hoping the Holy Alliance—a group of monarchies headed by the Emperors of Russia and Austria, and the King of Prussia—would help him regain his New World colonies.

Finally, Spain gave in and negotiated with Secretary of State John Quincy Adams the Florida, or Transcontinental, Treaty. Signed on February 22, 1819, it ceded Florida to the United States and established the boundary between the United States and Spanish territory from the Atlantic to the Pacific. The line zigzagged above Texas and New Mexico and to the Pacific along the northern boundaries of the present states of Utah, Nevada, and California. Samuel Flagg Bemis, the famed historian, wrote that Spain was prepared to cede Texas as well if Adams had pressed hard enough.[1] Adams wanted to, but President James Monroe was satisfied with less. As Bemis points out, the accession of Texas then would have avoided much of the distasteful difficulties with Mexico a few years later.

By 1820 it became apparent that Spanish rule on the mainland of America would soon be over. Weakened by the Napoleonic wars, without allies, Spain could no longer exert its rule over so great a distance. Simón Bolívar, after some early defeats, won great victories in what are now Venezuela, Colombia, Ecuador, and the state that bears his name, Bolivia. His armies were reinforced by about 5,000 Scots, English, and Irish soldiers whose careers in Europe had ended with the defeat of Napoleon. Their names have survived to this day via South American descendants who are Latin in all but name.

In Argentina José de San Martín raised a revolutionary

army and trained it to the finest European standards. In January 1817 he began an incredible adventure, marching his army across the Andes, dragging artillery 200 miles through mountain passes at an altitude of 12,000 feet. He surprised the Spaniards and freed Chile. San Martín then methodically prepared an assault on Peru, the heart of Spanish America, where Spanish forces were still strong. He raised a navy and occupied the Peruvian coast. In the meantime a liberal uprising in Spain had weakened the authority of the local viceroy. By mid-1821 rebellion spread and the viceroy moved his troops out of Lima into the interior. San Martín entered the city on July 9.

A year later San Martín met with Bolívar, who had fought his way across the top of the continent. They did not get along well and San Martín, one of the great liberators of human history, quietly bowed out, leaving South America to die in lonely exile in France in 1850. The field was left to Bolívar alone but it took him another two and a half years to conquer the Spaniards, with the republicans led in the final battle in December 1824 by Bolívar's finest soldier, General Antonio José de Sucre.

In Mexico independence came more quickly, though the circumstances were curious. In the rest of Latin America the fight for independence was led by liberal republicans, but in Mexico local control was held firmly by conservatives. When Ferdinand VII was overthrown in Spain, the Mexican conservatives refused to swear allegiance to a liberal government and, in 1821, declared independence.

But Bolívar's great triumph was only the prelude to frustration and disillusionment. He had destroyed Spanish power in Latin America but there was nothing to replace it with, no republican institutions—nothing except his own personal authority. It was not enough. Geography and the Spanish tradition of separatism caused his Greater Colombia to disintegrate into its component parts, Venezuela, Ecuador, and New Granada (now present-day Colombia and Panama). He, and the rulers of the other new states, had to resort to dictatorial rule to put down disorder, suspending constitutions and relying heavily upon the army. Thus, the father of Latin democracy became the first of the *caudillos,* a terrible irony. Another foreshadowing of the future presented itself. Bolívar's own nation, Colombia, borrowed large sums abroad but was unable to pay them. Disorder, with its effect on the economy, and the heavy expenses of maintaining a big army were too much for the infant state, a story that was to repeat itself time and again in Latin America.

Bolívar finally went into bitter exile, leaving behind these melancholy words: "There is no good faith in America, nor among the nations of America. Treaties are scraps of paper; constitutions, printed matter; elections, battles; freedom, anarchy; and life a torment." And just before he died he wrote, "America is ungovernable. He who serves a revolution ploughs the sea." [2]

There were changes in Portuguese America as well. The Prince Regent, Dom Joao, announced in 1815 that Brazil was now fully equal to Portugal and the next year he assumed the crown of both countries. Equal the two countries may have been, but the place for a Portuguese king was in Lisbon and in 1821, when Dom Joao's Portuguese throne seemed in jeopardy, he returned to Lisbon, leaving his son Pedro at Rio de Janeiro as Regent. Soon afterward it became evident that Portugal intended to return Brazil to its colonial status. Thus in September 1822 Dom Pedro proclaimed "Independence or death." [3] By the end of the year, with the enthusiastic support of Brazilian patriots, he had become Pedro I, Emperor of Brazil. But this was less revolution than an act of continuity, for there was little bloodshed.

In 1822 the United States began to recognize the new republics. The historic age of revolution was over, but in Latin America the real changes were few indeed. John Quincy Adams spoke these prophetic words: ". . . I wish well to their causes; but I have not yet seen and do not now see any prospect that they will establish free or liberal institutions of government. . . ." [4] A century and a half has passed and Adams' words are sadly almost as relevant today as when he uttered them. A fine analysis has been provided by Frank Tannenbaum, one of America's leading scholars on Latin America.

Independence abolished the monarchy but retained what is natural to monarchy—centralism, authoritarianism, and aristocracy— mainly because the revolutionists themselves were reared in the Spanish tradition and knew no other. Centralism, authoritarianism, and aristocracy could not be done away with, since no other way was known either to the leaders or the people. . . . The contrast between an authoritarian and a democratic society lies at this point. A democratic society finds it natural and logical to divide and distribute political authority in many places. No one person or institution is possessed of all the authority of the state. In an authoritarian society, quite the contrary is the case. . . . The president has no heir. There is no effective machinery in most countries for transferring the political power. This is the most serious crisis facing the elected chief executive. . . .

It is at this point that the independence movement served the people of Latin America poorly. It destroyed legitimate political authority without providing an equally legitimate substitute. When the wars of independence were over, no one knew where the political power resided. . . . The people of Latin America were left without a legitimate symbol of political authority. That vacuum has remained unfilled to this day. . . .[5]

Inseparable from the lack of accepted political institutions is the question of *personalismo* mentioned earlier. Tannenbaum also discusses that.

The great leader, by some magic, fraud, or force, has at his disposal all this power, and he cannot divide it, delegate it, or refuse to use it. As a matter of simple fact, he cannot resign it—as Fidel Castro couldn't resign from being the "maximum leader of the revolution" in Cuba. Castro could resign his office of Premier, but not his personal authority. The *caudillo* governs by his mere presence. . . .[6]

How different that is from the American experience. George Washington was the universal hero at the end of the American Revolution, yet he refused to be crowned. He could refuse because the British parliamentary system, which was the heritage of all the colonies' great leaders, provided for political institutions that were accepted by virtually everyone. Society could function without the "maximum leader." So concerned were the Founding Fathers with the concentration of power that they dispersed it even further—the famous "checks and balances"—between the federal government and the states and among the executive, legislative, and judicial branches at the national, state, and local levels. But the Latin American leaders, even those who genuinely believed in democracy, could not do that, for such generally accepted institutions simply did not exist.

The history of Latin America has been the constant, and as

yet largely unsuccessful, struggle to create such institutions for the exercise and transfer of power. The struggle has been long and difficult because those who have possessed the power have refused to give it up, systematically using every device possible to keep the masses from making effective use of their superior numbers. That struggle, simply stated, is the past, present, and future of Latin America.

But exactly who are those who have traditionally ruled Latin America, the oligarchies, as they have come to be known? Simply stated, the rulers have come from the aristocracy, a small percentage of the population that has always prided itself on its European ancestry, on the fact that they did not have to engage in physical labor, that they lived cultured lives and felt closer to Europe than to the people of their own lands. They derived their power from vast landholdings and the domination of commerce. And they were interrelated by ties of family, school, and tradition. With the government, the courts, the army, and most of the nation's wealth firmly in their hands, they were the tiny, elite apex atop an immense pyramid of plantation workers and laborers. There was virtually no middle class and what there was consisted largely of poor relatives of the upper class who were completely subservient to it. Only in recent decades has a middle class begun to emerge in Latin America with the development of modern industrial and commercial economies. And often the members of the new middle class want most of all to share the prerogatives of the upper class. Nonetheless, it is frequently idealists from the middle class who begin social and political movements that challenge the oligarchy. The most obvious example, of course, is Fidel Castro, a well-educated son of a middle-class family.

There have, to be sure, been changes in the oligarchy but they have come with glacial slowness. Occasionally members of the lower class force entry, almost always via the army. Men of drive and ambition, they soon recognize that the army is the only route out of the exploited lower classes. They enlist, work hard, and scheme, and if they are successful in rising to the higher ranks, more often by grabbing power than being promoted to it, the upper classes admit them, for they have understood from the beginning that the army is essential to their continuance in power. Occasionally others force their way into the oligarchy by way of the labor unions or student movements or political parties, but with few exceptions these new entrants do not want to change the power structure. They want to share in its wealth and privileges.

But what of revolutions, one asks, for everyone knows that Latin American history has been a bewildering succession of revolutions. That is true, but with only a few exceptions they have been revolutions in name not in fact. The word "revolution" seems to have some mystic appeal in Latin America. Its mere mention stirs the blood of many, and many are those who are veterans of numerous revolutions. Yet these revolutions are merely a struggle for power at the top, members of the oligarchy fighting among themselves and enlisting the masses, almost always poorly trained and armed, for their own selfish purposes. Sometimes a genuine "man of the people" leads the army in rebellion. But all too often, once he achieves power he becomes intoxicated by it and devotes his energies to self-enrichment and not to the betterment of the people from which he came.

There are stories almost without end of brave new revolutionaries coming to power in a flood of noble rhetoric, only to amass enormous personal fortunes wisely deposited in American or European banks. Indeed, politics by revolution has become a Latin American ritual, with each new leader allowing his unsuccessful predecessor to flee into luxurious exile abroad, for he knows that almost inevitably his time also will come. It has become accepted that life is pleasanter and infinitely more sensible if successive dictators are permitted to enjoy the fruits of their temporary triumphs. There are notable exceptions, of course, where leaders have been assassinated or executed, but the time-honored tradition has been comfortable exile.

So just as independence meant little to the Latin American masses, so, usually, have the so-called revolutions in which change has been limited to a change in the exploiters. The real revolutions in Latin America can be counted on the fingers of one hand. We shall discuss them as this narrative develops.

3

The Monroe Doctrine

B y 1825 all of Latin America, except Cuba and the Dominican Republic, was free of Spanish (and Portuguese) rule
either by armed revolution or by the simple collapse of Spanish power.

The United States was interested, of course. There were
practical reasons—geography and the hope for profitable commerce. There was the sympathy for new nations which had,
like the United States, won their independence from the Old
World. There was even the fairly widespread feeling that the
blessings of democracy "United States style" could best be dis-
tributed by joining some of the closer countries to the United
States—Cuba, perhaps Mexico and even the Dominican Republic. The aging Jefferson thought that Cuba "could be the
most interesting possible addition to our system of states." [1]
Aaron Burr was an open advocate of such expansion, and the
feeling persisted for nearly a century, until after the Spanish-
American War.

It was in this period that there developed the extraordinary

26

confidence that there was no limit to American achievement, that the United States had a unique mission to change the world. Related to it was the widespread belief that the American flag should fly over most of the continent, including Canada to the north and large parts of Latin America to the south. Even that was not enough for the most romantic of the American boosters. They believed that it was God's will that the Stars and Stripes flutter over the two continents from the Arctic to the Antarctic.

Great Britain also had an interest in Latin America, but there were no romantic elements to this interest. The interest was trade, the lifeblood of the British Empire. As Foreign Secretary George Canning saw it, "England will be a workshop and Latin America its farm." [2] The problem as he saw it was to exclude any possible rivals. Spain was too weak to cause much concern, but France was beginning to recover from the defeat of Napoleon and was again casting its eyes toward the New World. In March of 1823 Canning warned France not to attempt to seize any of Spain's former colonies. But he decided a warning was not enough and as England has always done, Canning looked for allies. The most obvious was the United States. Not only had Anglo-American relations improved steadily after the war of 1812, but the United States was clearly interested in keeping European countries out of Latin America. After some informal talks, Canning proposed in writing that the United States and Britain make a joint declaration along these lines:

1. We conceive the recovery of the Colonies by Spain to be hopeless.

2. We conceive the question of recognition of them, as Independent States, to be one of time and circumstances.

3. We are, however, by no means disposed to throw any impediment in the way of an arrangement between them and the mother country by amicable negotiations.

4. We aim not at the possession of any portion of them ourselves.

5. We could not see any portion of them transferred to any other Power, with indifference.[3]

The United States was interested but cautious. For one thing, it wanted immediate recognition of independence, and it was suspicious of British motives. Canning decided he could not wait for an American reply and simply notified France that Britain would not permit it to grab any of the former Spanish colonies. France recognized that such an action would be supremely difficult in view of Britain's great naval strength and, on October 9, 1823, informed Canning that she had no territorial ambitions in Spanish America.

Thus even before the Monroe Doctrine, one of the most significant documents in American history, it was clear to Secretary of State John Quincy Adams that Latin America was in no danger. Britain's navy would protect it from any other European power and Britain itself had disclaimed any territorial ambitions. Yet there was still the lingering fear in the mind of President Monroe and most of his associates that the Holy Alliance might intervene in the New World to assist Spain to regain its colonies. Monroe consulted two of his predecessors, Jefferson and Madison. Although Jefferson entirely agreed with George Washington's conviction that the United States should stay out of European affairs, he extended this to a belief that Europe should not be permitted to interfere in American affairs. He was for joining in the Anglo-American declaration even if the fourth paragraph of the proposed declaration reduced any possibility of annexing Cuba. Madison agreed and so did the entire Monroe Cabinet except Adams. He was convinced that the Holy Alliance would not dare to challenge the British Navy and that "it would be more candid, as well as more dignified, to avow our principles explicitly to Russia and France, than to come in as a cock-boat in the wake of the British man-of-war." Adams' advice prevailed, and it was decided that Monroe would state the American position in a presidential message on December 2, 1823.

Monroe asserted "as a principle in which the rights and interests of the United States are involved, that the American Continents, by the free and independent condition which they have assumed and maintain, are henceforth not to be considered as subjects for future colonization by any European Power. . . ." [4]

He pointed out that although the United States was always interested in events in Europe, "with which we have so much intercourse, and from which we derive our origin," it had never interfered in European affairs. He then made explicit his warning that Europe should not interfere in American affairs.

. . . It is only when our rights are invaded, or seriously menaced, that we resent injuries, or make preparations for our defense. With the movements in this Hemisphere we are of necessity more immediately connected, and by causes which must be obvious to all enlightened and impartial observers. The political system of the allied powers, is essentially different . . . from that of America. . . . We owe it therefore to candor, and to the amicable relations existing between the United States and those powers, to declare that we would consider any attempt on their part to extend their system to any portions of this Hemisphere, as dangerous to our peace and safety. With the existing Colonies or dependencies of any European power, we have not interfered, and shall not interfere. But with the Governments

who have declared their Independence, and maintained it, and
whose Independence we have, on great consideration, and on just
principles, acknowledged, we could not view any interposition for
the purpose of oppressing them, or controlling in any other manner,
their destiny, by any European power, in any other light, than as a
manifestation of an unfriendly disposition toward the United States.
. . . It is impossible that the allied powers should extend their political systems, to any portion of either continent, without endangering
our peace and happiness, nor can anyone believe, that our Southern
Brethren, if left to themselves, would adopt it of their own accord. It
is equally impossible, therefore, that we should behold such interposition in any form with indifference.[4]

This was a brilliant diplomatic stroke by Adams. Although
it was the British Navy that protected the new nations, the
United States got much of the credit. Since the Monroe Doctrine has played such a crucial, and dramatic, role in American history, it is necessary to determine just what it was. As
Henry Clay, Secretary of State in 1828, made clear, the Monroe Doctrine was the declaration "of the head of the Executive
Government of the United States. Although there is every reason to believe that the policy which it announced was in con-
formity with the opinion both of the nation and of Congress,
the declaration must be regarded as having been voluntarily
made, and not as conveying any pledge or obligation, the per-
formance of which foreign nations have a right to demand. . . ." [5]

In short, the Monroe Doctrine, as a unilateral declaration,
was binding on neither the United States nor anyone else. Nor
was it even approved by Congress. It was merely a statement,
with no legal character whatsoever. Contrast that with its interpretation in later periods, particularly by President John

Kennedy in the Cuban crises of 1961 and 1962.

Scholars have looked at it in various ways. The historian Samuel Bemis wrote that ". . . the announcement of the Monroe Doctrine was a courageous and independent act calculated to suit the policy of the United States rather than that of Great Britain. It is true that the Doctrine had no real force behind it. It was only a pronouncement, if you please, but it contained powerful words nevertheless, words that both served the immediate interests of the United States and exalted for the whole Hemisphere the ideals of independence and sovereignty of the people." [6] A somewhat less enthusiastic view was taken by another famous scholar, Dexter Perkins. "There can be no doubt at all . . . that Monroe's message of 1823 was directed against an illusory danger. There was never any fixed purpose to reconquer the Spanish colonies." [7] A more extreme view is offered by the Mexican scholar, no admirer of U.S. policy toward Latin America, Alonso Aguilar. He argues that the purpose of the Monroe Doctrine was not to help the people of the new nations but to establish the basis for U.S. dominance throughout the hemisphere. However it is interpreted, the Monroe Doctrine in its early years did not specify what the United States could do, only what European nations could not do. This, as we shall see, was to change.

There is no doubt, however, that the Monroe Doctrine, was largely ignored by just about everyone, the United States included, for years after its proclamation. When the United States quickly rejected the pleas of alliance from several Latin American states, the region soon decided that the United States did not intend any serious commitments to implement the Doctrine. And since it was apparent that the British Navy had the real military force, that Britain was a better source for loans and manufactured goods and as a market for raw materials, Britain became dominant in the region. It seized territory in Central America and the Falkland Islands off the tip of Argentina without any serious objection from the United States. As Bemis pointed out, "The history of the Monroe Doctrine shows plainly enough that its authority depends on what force the United States can use to back it up." [8]

While the Monroe Doctrine was languishing for several decades, another historic movement—that would eventually intersect with the Doctrine—was getting a halting start. Simón Bolívar hoped to found a league of Latin American nations and in 1826 called the Congress of Panama. Only four nations, Peru, Colombia, Mexico, and Central America (which later fragmented into several states) attended. The United States sent a delegation, but it left so late it arrived after the conference. Bolívar was premature. The new nations were still disorganized and were squabbling within and among themselves. Neither Britain nor the United States favored such an association then; they preferred to deal separately with weak, competing states. Yet Bolívar had an idea that has persisted to this day: that the Latin States with their common heritage and history should work together for the common good. Years later the United States seized on the idea of Pan-Americanism, beginning a debate that will no doubt continue for decades. Should the Latin states bind together with the United States or against it? To oversimplify somewhat, one school has argued that the United States has led the Pan-American movement for the welfare of both continents; the other argues that Pan-Americanism is just a device for U.S. domination. Both elements have no doubt existed simultaneously. The reader must determine for himself which has dominated at various times including, most importantly, today.

The Monroe Doctrine came briefly to life as the United States approached war with Mexico, a war that many historians argue was one of the less appealing chapters in American history. As we saw earlier, successive American presidents were concerned about Spanish colonies and claims along the frontiers of the young United States. The Louisiana territories became American via France, and Florida was annexed as Spain's power collapsed. When Mexico became independent in 1821, it, of course, assumed all the Spanish claims. By terms of the 1829 treaty signed by John Quincy Adams, Spanish (now Mexican) claims were enormous in what is now the United States: Texas, New Mexico, Arizona, Utah, Nevada, California, and parts of Colorado. The entire character of the United States and its history would have been profoundly different had it not gained this vast territory from Mexico. Although the American conquest of Mexico caused domestic dissent strikingly like that of the Vietnam War, it should be made clear that most of the territory seized by the United States would probably have gone to it eventually even without war. The reason has been well-expressed by Bernard DeVoto.

. . . it is a fundamental mistake to think of Mexico, in this period, or for many years before, as a republic or even as a government. It must be understood as a late stage in the breakdown of the Spanish Empire. Throughout that time it was never able to establish a stability, whether social or political. Abortive, discordant movements or revolution or counter-revolution followed one another in meaningless succession, and each one ran down in chaos from which no governing class ever arose, or even a political party, but only some gangs. . . . Furthermore, the portions of Mexico with which we are concerned, Texas, New Mexico, and California, were precisely the

portions where Spain's imperial energy had faltered and run down.
To this frontier Great Spain had come and here it could go no farther, here it began to ebb back.[9]

The dispute between the young United States and the even
younger Mexico began over Texas. When John Quincy
Adams became President, he tried, in 1827, to buy Texas for
$1 million, but Mexico turned him down. Texas was sparsely
populated, so Mexico offered large land grants to attract settlers. Most of them came from the United States and by the
time that Mexico realized the dangers, there was a large and
vigorous American colony. Mexico attempted to stop the flood
of American settlers, abolish slavery in the area, and rule the
Texans as Americans. It was too late. Most of the Texans
wanted the territory to join the United States. There was another attempt to buy Texas, this time by President Andrew
Jackson in 1829 for $5 million. Not only did he want Texas for
itself, but he wanted to end the increasing tension between the
young republics. Again the Mexicans refused. It may have
been foolish of them but it was certainly their right.

Under the leadership of Stephen F. Austin, the Texas Revolution broke out in 1835. The United States was officially neutral. But, as during the Latin American wars of independence
against Spain, the people were enthusiastic supporters of the
rebels. The legendary battle of the Alamo further stimulated
passions on both sides of the conflict. By early 1836 the Mexican government lost the struggle to put down the rebellion,
even though it repudiated the surrender treaty signed by General Santa Anna.

The successful rebellion raised tensions to the flash point.
Americans were outraged by the slaughter at the Alamo, and
the Mexicans were infuriated by what they saw as a land grab

by the *norteamericanos*. And many Mexicans were, no doubt, certain that the United States would not be satisfied with Texas. They were right.

Mexico declared that the annexation of Texas would mean war. Jackson believed them and refused to submit annexation legislation to Congress even though Texans and many Americans were clamoring for it. Martin Van Buren followed the same course, as did his successors, William Henry Harrison and, at first, John Tyler, the Vice-President who took office on Harrison's death. But when James K. Polk, an avowed annexationist, won the 1844 election, Tyler took that as a mandate for annexation, which he wanted to accomplish before Polk was inaugurated. He had tried some months earlier to push through an annexation treaty, only to have it rejected by the Senate, 35 to 16. He now tried another tactic, a joint resolution of Congress. On February 27, 1845, the Senate voted favorably, 27 to 25. The vote was not so close in the House, 132 to 76. Tyler signed the resolution on March 1, just three days before Polk took office. Polk immediately tried to buy California and New Mexico, which included almost all of the parts of Mexico now part of the United States. Mexico refused to sell.

It had been Tyler who had invoked the Monroe Doctrine in 1842 as Mexican-American tensions increased. In his annual message to Congress he said:

. . . Carefully abstaining from all interference in questions exclusively referring themselves to the political interests of Europe, we may be permitted to hope an equal exemption from the interference of European Governments in what relates to the States of the American continent.[10]

This was a foreshadowing of later use of the Monroe Doctrine. Tyler was asking for hands off, not to protect a Latin

American state from a European state, but to prevent a European nation from helping a Latin state involved in a controversy with the United States.

When Tyler signed the joint resolution, Mexico, despite its earlier threats, did not declare war. But it did increase the fervor of its diplomatic protests. On July 4 (doubtless not a coincidence) a convention of Texans ratified the action of the Texas Congress in approving annexation. A couple of weeks later Mexico passed a declaration of war to take effect whenever the United States annexed Texas or sent federal troops there. Polk sent General Zachary Taylor (Old Rough and Ready) with a contingent of troops to Corpus Christi on the western bank of the Nueces River, just inside territory claimed by Mexico. On December 29, 1845, Texas became the twenty-eighth state of the Union. But still Mexico held off.

Polk wanted the Mexicans to strike first. They did not at the Nueces, so Taylor was ordered deeper into territory claimed by Mexico, south and west to the Rio Grande. One of the officers was young Lieutenant Ulysses S. Grant, later Union commander in the Civil War and President. He wrote in his *Memoirs:* "I was bitterly opposed to . . . the war . . . as one of the most unjust ever waged by a stronger against a weaker nation. . . . We were sent to provoke a fight, but it was essential that Mexico should commence it. . . . Mexico showing no willingness to come to the Nueces to drive the invaders from her soil, it became necessary for the 'invaders' to approach within a convenient distance to be struck."

Grant was not the only member of Taylor's army to dissent. Lieutenant Ethan Allen Hitchcock wrote: "As to the right of this movement, I have said from the first that the United States are the aggressors. We have outraged the Mexican Gov-

ernment and people by an arrogance and presumption that
deserve to be punished. . . . My heart is not in this unholy
business; I am against it from the bottom of my soul as a most
unholy and unrighteous proceeding; but, as a military man, I
am bound to execute orders." [11]

The same issues arose then that were to arise more than a
century later in the Vietnam War. The invasion into Mexican
territory was denounced in similar terms by such famous
American writers as Henry David Thoreau and Ralph Waldo
Emerson. And among the dissenters was a young congressman
from Illinois, Abraham Lincoln.

The war that Polk wanted so he could win California was
not far off. On April 26, 1846, a Mexican general sent a large
force across the Rio Grande. Taylor sent out some scouts. The
two unequal forces clashed. Seventeen Americans were killed
and all the rest but one, who escaped to tell the story, were
captured. War had begun. But because of poor communications, an impatient Polk was unaware of this and was trying to
decide if Congress would declare war even if Mexico did not
strike first. Once the word got to Washington, however, Polk
moved quickly. On May 11, two days after receiving Taylor's
message, Polk asked Congress to declare war, asserting that
". . . after reiterated menace, Mexico has passed the boundary of the United States, has invaded our territory, and shed
American blood upon the American soil." [12] Certainly sufficient cause for war—if events were as Polk reported them,
but his account was immediately challenged.

As senators and representatives were quick to point out,
there was considerable doubt that the skirmish took place on
American soil. Some argued that the territory north of the Rio
Grande to the Nueces River was disputed territory, that Mex-

ico had never conceded that the Rio Grande was the Texas boundary, and that Texans had never controlled the territory. Other lawmakers asserted that the territory was not even in dispute, that the United States had absolutely no claim to it, and that by sending Taylor and his army to the Rio Grande, he, Polk, had been the one guilty of aggression.

But whoever owned the soil, American blood had been spilled, and as history has demonstrated many times before and since, people of any nation seldom stop to think or ask many questions at a time like that. The House voted war that very day, 173 to 14, and the Senate the next day, 40 to 2.

Polk moved quickly to prosecute the war. Perhaps all wars are chaos; this one certainly was. Orders, often faulty from the beginning, took weeks, sometimes months, to reach commanders in the field. Often they were flagrantly disobeyed. The President and his top commanders, Taylor and Winfield T. Scott, openly exchanged criticism, and generals disputed one another in the newspapers. Even Polk's ambassador refused to come home from Mexico City when he was twice ordered to. Nonetheless, the United States won the war easily. Poor Mexico was totally disorganized, much more so than even the United States. Its troops were just as brave and more numerous than the Americans, but they were poorly led and terribly equipped. On May 8, even before war was declared, Taylor had won a great victory, depending mainly on his far superior artillery. Another, even greater, victory was won the next day at Resaca de la Palma.

By fall 1846 Taylor had put together a string of victories that both pleased Polk and alarmed him, for the Democrat Polk thought the Whig Taylor had his eye on the White House. Polk wanted a politically more acceptable general to make the final assault on Mexico City but Scott, the army commander in Washington and clearly the most competent general, was also a Whig. There was a long pause in the war while Polk chafed at the refusal of the Mexicans to give in, even though it was obvious that they didn't have a chance. By early 1847 it was apparent that the Mexicans would give up only if their capital were captured. Reluctantly Polk recognized that the only alternative to Taylor was Scott. Scott happily took the field command and with it most of Taylor's army. Taylor was bitter, so now there was not only hostility between the top two generals on the one hand and the President on the other, but between the two generals themselves, with Taylor refusing to talk to his superior.

Not only did Taylor refuse to meet with Scott but he disobeyed specific orders that he remain on the defense while Scott began his campaign. Instead of staying put, Taylor moved toward Santa Anna, who outnumbered him nearly four to one. Santa Anna decided to polish off Taylor and then turn his attention to Scott. It was a good idea. Santa Anna, however, pushed his men so hard on a forced march through bad weather that they arrived exhausted. When he found Taylor dug in in a superb defensive position, Santa Anna on Washington's birthday pushed the attack immediately instead of giving his men time to rest or swinging around Taylor and capturing his base camp at Saltillo. Nonetheless, it was a near thing. The Mexicans fought bravely despite terrible casualties meted out by Taylor. The battle raged for two days, with the Mexicans capturing some vital American artillery. Both sides suffered heavy losses and the Americans feared a third day of resolute attack would mean their defeat. But Santa Anna, to the disgust of his men, withdrew and when the third day dawned, the exhausted and nearly defeated Americans found the field to themselves. They shouted for joy. Almost certain defeat had been turned into victory. Santa Anna had suffered cruel losses that handicapped him in the subsequent campaign against Scott, yet he had not gained the victory that would have given the Mexicans momentum and confidence. It was Taylor's last fight but it ensured him the presidency.

The final thrust was Scott's and it was a superb campaign. On March 9 at Vera Cruz, Scott made the first amphibious landing in modern warfare, rowboats carrying soldiers to shore under protective Navy guns. He laid seige to Vera Cruz, finally capturing the walled city with the loss of only nineteen lives. In April, Scott met Santa Anna for the first time, inflicting a costly defeat. Prominent in that battle and in the entire campaign was Robert E. Lee, who was often cited in generals' reports. And there were dozens of other future Civil War generals who received their training with Taylor and Scott.

By August, reinforcements had brought Scott's army up to 10,000 and he began the final push on Mexico City. It was a bold campaign, for he had neither bases nor a supply line. He had to live on the country. On August 20, Scott won a costly victory against Santa Anna with more than a thousand U.S. dead, wounded, or missing. On September 8, the Americans began the assault on the fiercely-defended fortified city, and after six terrible days of fighting a contingent of U.S. marines marched into "the halls of Montezuma." Santa Anna fled and the war was over.

The peace negotiations took months, but on February 2, 1848 the Treaty of Guadalupe Hidalgo was signed, surrendering California and New Mexico to the United States. In return the United States paid $15 million and assumed up to $3¼ million the claims of American citizens against Mexico. Now the United States stretched "from sea to shining sea," possessed of vast lands of almost limitless wealth. But there can be no doubt that the United States grabbed these lands from its neighbor by force of arms, lands that almost certainly would have eventually fallen into American hands anyway because a young, disorganized Mexico did not have the strength to govern them.

While Polk's main preoccupations in the foreign field were the Mexican War and the negotiations with Great Britain that established the present states of Oregon and Washington, he had to cast an occasional anxious eye toward Latin America where the Monroe Doctrine was continuing to pile up precedents of nonapplication. The United States had ignored French interventions in 1838 in the United Provinces of the Plata (now Argentina) and Mexico. Even more serious was the Anglo–French invasion of the Plata River region from 1845 to 1849. Polk flatly told Argentina that he would not help it or Uruguay in any way. Concerned with the Mexican situation, Polk was not about to get involved with two powerful European nations over the fate of two Latin nations thousands of miles away. This reinforces the obvious interpretation that the Monroe Doctrine was not regarded in Washington as an invariable policy, but that it was to be invoked only if U.S. interests were involved and if the United States had sufficient power. The Doctrine was not something that Latin American nations could rely on for their protection; it was solely for the convenience of the United States.

Polk was also involved in another event that did not seem so important at the time but proved to be of great consequence more than a half century later. The Republic of New Granada (now Colombia and Panama) was alarmed over the increasing British presence in Central America. It appealed to the United States, offering in return for a guarantee of its sovereignty transit rights across the Isthmus of Panama. The U.S. minister, although he had no instructions on this question (it must be remembered that since mail took weeks and even months in those days, diplomats were given much more authority than they possess today), signed the Bidlack Treaty of 1846. With it the United States guaranteed "the rights of sovereignty and of property which New Granada has and possesses over the said territory." We shall see later how well Theodore Roosevelt would respect this treaty.

This, of course, was the first step toward the Panama Canal, although in those days it was land transit across the narrow isthmus dividing the Atlantic and Pacific oceans that was important. The treaty arrived in Washington in the first year of the Mexican War. Polk immediately perceived its importance. When California became part of the Union, it would be far easier to sail down the Atlantic to Panama, cross overland and sail up the Pacific to California than it would be to cross the immense North American continent with its deserts and mountains. Yet so ingrained was the U.S. reluctance to join in "entangling alliances," even with another American nation, that Polk was reluctant to submit it to the Senate. Finally its importance overcame his hesitation and he urged the Senate to ratify it. The Senate, too, was hesitant and delayed so long that New Granada sent a special mission to urge its ratification. But when Mexico ceded California to the United States, the Senate, too, perceived its importance and ratified it on June 8, 1848 by a vote of 29 to 7.

Now it was Britain's turn to become alarmed. For political

and commercial reasons, it wanted to restrict U.S. influence in the area, so it attempted to gain transit rights in Nicaragua. The contest came to a head under President Taylor, who was preoccupied by the bitter struggle between the slave and antislave states that would lead to the Civil War. As Samuel Bemis put it, "Both Governments found it desirable to compromise, the United States because it faced the danger of civil war at home, Great Britain if only because undefended Canada was a hostage for the beneficent conduct of the British navy toward the United States." [13]

Since the isthmus was more important to the United States, it made the greater concession. According to the Clayton-Bulwer Treaty of 1850, any railway or canal of the future would be under the joint control of the United States and Britain. This, of course, was a specific denial of the Monroe Doctrine, and not in remote Falkland Islands or the Rio Plata region but in a nearby area crucial to United States interests. Nonetheless, the treaty did prevent Britain from taking advantage of the Civil War to establish complete dominance over Central America.

In 1853, the danger of civil war seemed to have retreated, so the new President, Democrat Franklin Pierce, again invoked the substance of the Monroe Doctrine because of British territorial acquisitions in Central America. In his inaugural address he declared that "the rights, security, and repose of this Confederacy reject the idea of interference or colonization on this side of the ocean by any foreign power beyond present jurisdiction as utterly inadmissible." [14] Congress may well have agreed with Pierce but, as with Monroe's historic statement, it took no legislative action to demonstrate its support. Pierce's speech sparked the controversy, and in London, Lord Clarendon declared to the American minister that the Monroe Doctrine was only the "dictum of the distinguished personage who announced it, and not . . . an international axiom which ought to regulate the conduct of European states." [15]

For six years the two nations squabbled, and finally in 1859 Britain returned the Bay Islands to Honduras and the Mosquito Coast to Nicaragua. Fortunately the start of the Civil War held off long enough for Britain to make these concessions, but as soon as the war did break out Britain formally declared that British Honduras was a crown colony, a blatant challenge to the Monroe Doctrine.

President James Buchanan also invoked the Monroe Doctrine in 1859 and 1860 when he proposed the occupation of Mexico. Mexican monarchists and the Church were flirting with the idea of getting some European monarch to sit on a Mexican throne, an idea violently opposed by Mexican liberals. In his 1859 annual message to Congress Buchanan asserted that Mexico was "a wreck upon the ocean, drifting about as she is impelled by different factions. As a good neighbor shall we not extend to her a helping hand to save her? If we do not it would not be surprising should some other nation undertake the task, and thus force us to interfere at last, under circumstances of increased difficulty, for the maintenance of our established policy." [16]

But the North recognized this solicitude for what it was: designs on Mexico which, if annexed, would mean several more slave states, strengthening proslavery forces in the Senate. Thus, the Northern senators opposed him and Buchanan's plans came to nothing. He was right, however, in predicting that European power would intervene in Mexico.

4
Asserting the Doctrine

When the Civil War broke out in 1861, the no-longer *United* States was forced to turn its attention inward for four anguished years. The European monarchies took advantage of this situation to engage in an extraordinary adventure, romantic even, in a futile sort of way. The French Revolution having been temporarily sidetracked again, Napoleon III, nephew of Napoleon Bonaparte, was on the throne. He conspired with the fellow monarchies of Britain and Spain to put the Austrian Archduke Ferdinand Maximilian on the throne of the ancient Montezumas in Mexico. With the United States tearing itself asunder, the Monroe Doctrine was obviously no handicap.

Circumstances in Mexico also seemed favorable. The country, as usual in its early decades, was torn with dissension. The conservative royalists, powerful since independence, had long wanted to find a European prince to put on a nonexistent Mexican throne. When President Benito Juárez, a liberal who had already attacked the privileges of the established church and army, decided to suspend payments on foreign debts, this provided a pretext for European intervention. Juárez has a place in Mexican history similar to his American contemporary, Abraham Lincoln. Like Lincoln, he was a man of humble birth, a full-blooded Zapotec Indian. He, too, struggled for an education and became a lawyer, was devoted to the common people and dedicated himself to national unity.

In 1864, Archduke Maximilian and a host of French troops sailed merrily off for Mexico on British and Spanish ships. His reception on landing was less than enthusiastic, with Mexican pro-Republican forces opposing the advance of French troops to the capital. But the French, for the moment, were too strong and Maximilian arrived in Mexico City to the delight of Mexican aristocrats and the Church hierarchy. The British and the Spanish began to have second thoughts. Although they had used the same pretext for intervention that President Buchanan had urged for U.S. intervention—damages to their nationals—the adventure began to seem less attractive.

Since both the North and the South protested, Britain recognized that after the Civil War was over there would be a reckoning and that British Canada was wholly unprotected against any possible American strike. The Spanish, although they were unregenerate monarchists, would have preferred a Bourbon to a Hapsburg on the throne of their former colony. Also Spain was fully occupied in its futile attempt to reconquer the Dominican Republic. So both countries pulled out, leaving France as Maximilian's sole support. It wasn't enough as Benito Juárez, who had fled the capital to carry on guerrilla warfare, put increasing pressure on the French puppet. The adventure was buckling of its own weight. Then when the American Civil War ended, the United States increased its protests, backing them up by sending 25,000 veteran troops to the Rio Grande under the command of the redoubtable cavalry leader, General Philip Sheridan. In 1866, Secretary of State William Seward demanded of Paris a timetable for the withdrawal of French troops. With Juárez growing in strength, with the Americans at the border, Napoleon III recognized the hopelessness of his wild dream. The last French soldier departed in the spring of 1867. The Monroe Doctrine had had a rebirth. But poor Maximilian had a quick death. He was captured by Juárez, court-martialed, and shot.

At long last the Monroe Doctrine was no longer a "paper tiger." Although the European nations would accord it no legal standing—for it had none—they respected it. The leading scholar of the Monroe Doctrine, Dexter Perkins, put it: "It had become a true national dogma, endorsed by all parties, awakening an instantaneous response in the breasts of patriotic Americans." [1]

For some years after the Civil War, the United States lost its appetite for expansion. It wanted to bind the wounds of war, settle the vast lands in the West won from Mexico and negotiated from Britain; it wanted to concentrate on its extraordinary economic growth, but there were spurts of interest, to be sure.

President Ulysses S. Grant broadened the Monroe Doctrine in his annual message to Congress, in December 1869, when he said that European dependencies in the Americas were "no longer regarded as subject to transfer from one European power to another. When the present relationship of colonies ceases, they are to become independent powers, exercising the right of choice and self-control in the determination of their future condition and relation with other powers." [2] Again this declaration had no legal standing, but it clearly indicated an increased American conviction that the Western Hemisphere was its sphere of influence.

Grant did have some ideas of acquisition but he was blocked by the Senate. His personal agent had negotiated a treaty of annexation with the Dominican Republic in 1870, but the Senate declined to ratify it. It is futile but interesting to speculate what might have happened had the United States annexed the Dominican Republic. Would that have whetted its appetite for Haiti and Cuba or even revived the interest in persuading Canada to join the Union?

Curiously, just as the mystique of the Monroe Doctrine was growing in the United States, in Latin America began the growth of sentiment for a doctrine of nonintervention in the New World. And the Pan-American idea began to show signs of rebirth. All of the movements would intersect time and again. The first step toward nonintervention was the widespread belief among Latin American nations that foreign residents should be subject to local courts and not be able to seek recourse from their home governments. This, of course, is inarguable—in theory at least. No one would expect an Englishman residing in New York, say, to be able to refuse to comply with the judgment of New York courts and turn to London for help, if he had been treated in the same manner as an American citizen. However, foreigners argued that in those chaotic times Latin American courts were often prejudiced against aliens and did not treat them fairly. Only by appealing to their home government could they get justice. Latin Americans, on the other hand, argued that aliens often tried to avoid proper judgments by appealing to their own government. Since these appeals sometimes resulted in the dispatch of a for-

eign gunboat or the landing of a contingent of troops, it is easy
to see why Latin Americans objected. But since it was true
that local courts were often unfair, the question was a difficult
one. It was one that would be discussed for three-quarters of a
century.

Towards the end of the nineteenth century another impetus
for nonintervention developed. The Latin nations began to
recognize that while the United States might protect them
from Europe, there was no one to protect them from the
United States.

For a while in the 1880s there seemed a potential threat to
the Monroe Doctrine when Ferdinand de Lesseps, a French-
man who had built the Suez Canal, began to build one
through the Isthmus of Panama. President Rutherford B.
Hayes declared that there should be a canal under American
control. In 1881, Secretary of State James G. Blaine said that
the control of an Isthmian canal by a European power would
be a violation of the Monroe Doctrine. France quickly pointed
out that the canal was under private not governmental control. Britain responded that the Clayton-Bulwer Treaty of
1850 had settled the matter. But the issue died when yellow
fever prevented the completion of the canal.

In 1889, the first real Pan-American Conference was held.
One had been called in 1881 by Secretary of State James G.
Blaine, but for a number of reasons it fell through. President
Grover Cleveland issued another call in 1888 and the republics of the Western Hemisphere met in Washington in late
1889, but under the sponsorship of Benjamin Harrison, who
had defeated Cleveland in the electoral vote even though he
had received fewer popular votes. Blaine was again Secretary
of State and he presided over this first International Confer-

ence of American States, now better known as Pan-American Conferences.

Although few of the many recommendations in the political and economic fields were ratified by the respective governments, the Conference did establish the International Office of the American Republics, later known as the Pan American Union. At first it had limited functions and for some while it was under the exclusive direction of the United States. Later, however, it was placed under the joint control of the twenty-one American republics as the permanent, official center of the Pan-American movement. While it had no authority over its member states, it provided the organizational basis of Pan-Americanism and later became the Secretariat of the Organization of American States. The United States has been the dominant member to this day, although there are signs that its influence has begun to diminish somewhat.

More important at the time, on the eve of what has been termed America's Age of Imperialism, was the dispute between Venezuela and Great Britain settled by the intervention of Cleveland, who had returned to the White House by defeating Harrison in their second contest. The dispute was about the boundary between Venezuela and British Guiana, where gold had been discovered in 1884. Venezuela appealed to the United States to arbitrate. Cleveland decided that the matter fell within the scope of the Monroe Doctrine. The question was not the justice of British claims, but whether or not it would attempt to gain its desires by virtue of its superior strength compared with Venezuela. After some inconclusive haggling between London and Washington, Cleveland instructed his Secretary of State, Richard Olney, to find out once and for all if Britain would agree to arbitration. It was a good moment for a tough American stand, for once again U.S. interests were favored by developments in Europe. Britain was separated from France and Russia, at odds with Germany, and on the verge of the Boer War in South Africa. As the American Ambassador wrote to Washington early in 1895, "Great Britain has just now her hands full in other quarters of the globe. The United States is the last nation on earth with whom the British people or their rulers desire to quarrel, and of this I have new proofs every day in my intercourse with them." [3]

So Secretary Olney took a hard line. On June 20, 1895 he sent a message to the American Ambassador to be handed to Lord Salisbury, British Prime Minister and Foreign Secretary. It was a definition of the Monroe Doctrine that Washington has accepted to this day. Olney associated the dispute with the Monroe Doctrine and asserted that the Doctrine was linked with the security of the United States and the cause of self-determination in the entire Western Hemisphere. He took a high moral tone and informed Britain that the Doctrine was "a doctrine of American public law, well founded in principle and abundantly sanctioned by precedent, which entitles and requires the United States to treat as an injury to itself the forcible assumption by a European power of political control over an American state." But Olney did not rest his argument on that statement alone. Another section of his message was less than diplomatic.

Today the United States is practically sovereign on this continent, and its fiat is law upon the subjects to which its confines its interposition. Why? It is not because of the pure friendship or good will felt for it. It is not simply by reason of its high character as a civilized state, nor because wisdom and justice and equity are the invariable

characteristics of the dealings of the United States. It is because, in addition to all other grounds, its infinite resources combined with its isolated position render it master of the situation and practically invulnerable as against any or all other powers.[4]

In short, the Western Hemisphere was the U.S. sphere of influence and no one could do anything about it. Lord Salisbury did not entirely agree. He replied: "The Government of the United States is not entitled to affirm as a universal proposition with reference to a number of independent states for whose conduct it assumes no responsibility, that its interests are necessarily concerned in whatever may befall those states simply because they are situated in the Western Hemisphere." [5]

Salisbury was agreeing with an assertion made during the first Pan-American Conference by the President of Argentina, Roque Sáenz Peña. This is what he said about the Monroe Doctrine:

In its legal aspect, this declaration does not amount to a doctrine; it is an action, but not a system or an international or political theory. . . .

Since the New World is made up of free and independent republics, not one of them, so far, has achieved sufficient international stature to represent the rest, or to determine their destinies with relation to the Old World. That imaginary line which seeks to perpetuate itself on the waters dividing two continents, is not a doctrine but a parody of the famous encyclical which divided the world into two parts, conferring flimsy and precarious sovereignties over them.

The Argentinian statesman then went on to anticipate criticism directed against the United States often during the twentieth century, and to anticipate numerous U.S. interventions.

The statements on the political system of the peoples of America could not be graver . . . they entail curtailment of their autonomous powers to choose the forms of government best suited to their natures, interests, and sociological conditions without being pressed into the particular mold of one nation which exercised the same right when it was constituted, as the others now demand and exercise. . . . In the name of what principle could such intervention for the purpose of dictating the political organization of the new states be justified? Were they even consulted? Did there happen to have been a continental plebiscite which consecrated the institutional system of the Republic of the North to be extended and spread throughout a hemisphere? [6]

However justified these criticisms of the Monroe Doctrine may have been, such was not the view in the United States. Cleveland made an issue of Salisbury's reply that aroused Congress, the press, and the public. When London learned of the American response, it was appalled. With Britain isolated in Europe, it wanted American friendship, not the prospect of conflict over the borders of a distant colony. Salisbury agreed to arbitration, and the award on October 3, 1899 was not much different than Britain had claimed except that Guiana did not extend to the banks of the Orinoco River as the British had wanted. Nearly a century later, the matter is still being disputed by Venezuela and the now-independent nation of Guyana.

Despite Secretary of State Olney's claims and despite the unquestioned strength of the United States in the Western Hemisphere, the Monroe Doctrine was still only the declaration of a President. And even if Congress had affirmed it, it still would have been a unilateral declaration, not a treaty, and it was still challenged within the hemisphere and without.

Its force rested solely on force. Nonetheless, despite the fact that it had no standing in international law, Bemis was correct in describing it in these terms:

So great a hold did the Doctrine have on popular imagination by the end of the century, so sacred a formula had it become for the future policy of the United States, that it would be easy for a future President to invoke it in good faith as an instrument of protective imperialism and in so doing bring the Latin American policy of the United States to a parting of the ways.[7]

We shall soon see how just that took place.

5

The Dawn of Imperialism

Although there had been occasional ventures outside the United States, the first century of this nation's history was primarily concerned with establishing what Bemis liked to call the Continental Republic. Dealings with Britain, Spain, and France had concentrated on the vast lands outside the original thirteen colonies that eventually became part of what is now the United States. But as the end of the nineteenth century neared, that phase was over. Even the immense lands of the western frontier were filling up. Industrialization had come to the United States with a rush, and now it was widely believed that American industrialists would have to seek foreign markets. Perhaps most important of all, there was a new spirit abroad in the land.

Personified by Theodore Roosevelt, such senators as Henry Cabot Lodge and Albert J. Beveridge and the great naval strategist, Captain Alfred T. Mahan, there was a heady feeling that America should take its place all over the world with the other great nations. That it should have a splendid Navy, pos-

sessions in the Caribbean and the Pacific, that it should carry
out the American destiny to spread the blessings of democracy
and civilization the world over. Not untypical of the rhetoric
of the expansionists was this statement by Senator Beveridge.

. . . The trade of the world must and shall be ours. . . . We will
cover the ocean with our merchant marine. We will build a navy to
the measure of our greatness. . . . Our institutions will follow the
flag on the wings of our commerce. And American law, American
order, American civilization, and the American flag, will plant
themselves on shores hitherto bloody and benighted, but by those
agencies of God henceforth to be made beautiful and bright.[1]

In the campaign of 1896 the Republicans, who would occupy the White House until after Woodrow Wilson's election
in 1912, advanced a vigorous foreign policy. They wanted Ha-
waii and the Danish West Indies and an American canal
across Central America. They reasserted "the Monroe Doctrine in its full extent" and urged that the United States use its
good offices to restore peace in Cuba and give it independence.

Again American eyes were cast on Cuba. There were still
those who were convinced that Cuba, only 90 miles offshore,
was a natural part of the United States, and who believed that
Canada would peacefully decide to join the union. So it was
Cuba that was to change the course of American history and
thus become so related to this nation that our destinies have
been intertwined ever since.

Cuba had been the only Spanish colony not to rebel in the
early 1800s, but by mid-century an independence movement
had developed there as well. Insurrection broke out in 1868
and continued for ten years, finally put down by the harshest
repression. Although the United States was naturally sympa-

thetic to the rebels, it offered no substantial help, being more concerned at the time with binding its wounds after the Civil War. But the independence movement simmered for decades and began to boil toward the end of the century, with Cuba's national hero, José Martí, serving in exile as its poet, propagandist, symbol, and fund raiser. Martí led a band of exiles on a return to Cuba in 1895 and although he was soon killed by the Spaniards, the Cuban patriots began a guerrilla war from their bases in the mountains, just as Fidel Castro was to do a half century later.

Again the Spaniards responded harshly, hoping to put down the rebellion by brute strength and fear. Spain sent to Cuba the able but ruthless Captain-General Valeriano Weyler, whose tactics soon earned him in the American press the name of "Butcher." His tactic, "reconcentration," was new then but it was to be used in later wars, and critics of American policy in Vietnam have accused the United States of similar tactics.

. . . If the rebels would not fight in the open field, he would herd their women, children, and old people into cities and towns, construct elaborate defenses, and systematically reduce the countryside until it would not support the insurrection. It was a brutal method that inflamed American public opinion, the press, the pulpit, and government. A later generation, inured to the prospect of total annihilation, may find this hard to believe; but that era's concept of war did not encompass the destruction of non-military property, ravagement of whole provinces, and murder of non-combatants.[2]

Although Cleveland, in his last term, shared the national sentiment, he did not want war with Spain. He thought a peaceful settlement was possible and he pressed Spain to make the genuine reforms in Cuba that might bring peace. But

Spain refused and finally Cleveland got angry. He did not want to commit the incoming William McKinley administration but he could not refrain from saying in his last annual message on December 7, 1896 that "the spectacle of the utter ruin of an adjoining country, by nature one of the most fertile and charming on the globe, would engage the serious attention of the Government and people of the United States in any circumstances." And the outgoing President warned: ". . . the United States is not a nation to which peace is a necessity." [3]

Although McKinley was a Republican, the party of "hawks" on Cuba, to use a term born in a later Cuban crisis, he, too, wanted peace. But the jingoist press of William Randolph Hearst and Joseph Pulitzer clamored for war and even such presumably responsible figures as Teddy Roosevelt seemed to think a little whiff of gunpowder would be good for the American character. Nonetheless, it seemed for a while that McKinley would succeed in avoiding war. He, like Cleveland, pressed Spain for reforms in Cuba and they seemed to be forthcoming. A new Spanish government recalled Weyler, relaxed the reconcentration policy, and said further reforms were on the way. But when the new policy was announced, it seemed more of the same and the American press increased its warlike clamor, inventing Spanish atrocity stories if the real things weren't gory enough.

By early 1898 things were getting out of hand. Anti-autonomy riots broke out in Cuba, indicating that even if Madrid were prepared to make concessions, the Spanish colonists were not. Still worse was yet to come. The impetus toward war was increased by one of the great diplomatic scandals in American history. The Spanish minister to Washington, Dupuy de Lôme, had written a fearfully indiscreet letter in which he expressed his low opinion of President McKinley. It somehow fell into the hands of rebel supporters who wasted no time in getting it to friendly newspapers. On February 9 readers of the New York *Journal* were startled to see this headline: WORST INSULT TO THE UNITED STATES IN ITS HISTORY. Whether the facts justified such a categorical headline or not, American readers certainly were not pleased to read the Spanish minister's description of McKinley as "weak and a bidder for the admiration of the crowd, besides being a would-be politician who tries to leave the door open behind himself while keeping on good terms with the jingoes of his party."

But even that choice morsel for the jingoist "yellow" newspapers was soon overwhelmed by what was to happen a week later. On January 25 the battleship *Maine*, pride of the American fleet, had steamed into the Havana harbor on a "friendly visit," a less than subtle pressure on Spain to carry out genuine reforms in Cuba. Spanish officials were careful to greet the *Maine* cordially, but then at 9:40 on the evening of February 15 the great battleship exploded, killing 260 of the crew. Even though subsequent investigation was never able to determine whether the explosion was an accident or deliberate, the American press immediately raised the slogan that was to become the battle cry of the invading Americans a few months later: "Remember the Maine!"

McKinley still hoped for peace, but he decided that if war were coming the United States had better be prepared. He asked Congress for $50 million for defense, an enormous sum in those distant days. Congress swiftly responded and the Spanish were shocked. As the American minister cabled from Madrid, "It has not excited the Spaniards, it has simply stunned them. To appropriate fifty million out of money in the treasury, without borrowing a cent, demonstrates wealth and power. Even Spain can see this. To put the money without restrictions at your disposal demonstrated entire confidence in you by all parties. The Ministry and press are simply stunned." [4]

McKinley increased the pressure on Madrid and the war supporters increased the pressure on McKinley. The once-popular President was the subject of bitter attacks. He finally sent an ultimatum to Madrid: grant an armistice, undertake massive relief works; if peace terms not reached by October McKinley would arbitrate. Implicit was the stand that Cuba must ultimately be independent. In early April the American minister cabled from Madrid that Spain was giving in, but McKinley could wait no longer and on April 11 sent a war message to Congress. Historians are still arguing over whether the war was necessary. Some say that Spain had waited too long, that the momentum toward war was irresistible. Others argue that if McKinley had waited just a little longer, he could have gotten all he needed to convince the American people that war was not necessary.

But necessary or not, war it was. Volunteers flocked to the colors by the tens of thousands as if war were a glorious adventure, or perhaps it is until it is experienced. But as usual, just as in the Mexican War, confusion reigned in Washington and in Florida, where the expeditionary force assembled. But while the Army struggled to reduce chaos to manageable proportions, the Navy struck for a sudden and historic victory. Teddy Roosevelt, who was Assistant Secretary of the Navy, had taken advantage of his superior's absence one day in February to order Admiral George Dewey to prepare the Pacific fleet to capture the Philippines. He got the fleet ready and on April 24

McKinley gave the order. Dewey steamed out of Hong Kong on April 29 and at about midnight on April 30 sailed, strangely unopposed, past the Spanish guns at the entrance to the great Manila harbor. At 4:00 A.M. the officers and men of the American fleet had coffee and hardtack. Soon thereafter the Spanish fleet was spotted, its battle flags flying in the morning breeze. Dewey sailed right at it and at 5:41 A.M. gave his famous order: "You may fire when ready, Gridley." Five hours later the brave but outgunned Spanish fleet was silent. In Manila George Dewey had won a historic battle in the war over Cuba, half a world away. In that moment America had become an imperial power, its first imperial outpost an island nation that few Americans knew anything about.

The victory in Cuba took more time. The American Army wasn't ready to invade until June 22. When they did, there was bitter fighting with the Spaniards at first putting up stiff resistance. The Americans fought well. Teddy Roosevelt's charge at the head of his Rough Riders not only got him San Juan Hill but, eventually, the White House as well. It is notable that several black regiments fought with distinction. Frank Knox, who was Franklin Roosevelt's Navy Secretary during World War II, became separated from Teddy's Rough Riders "but I joined a troop of the Tenth Cavalry, colored, and for a time fought with them shoulder to shoulder, and in justice to the colored race I must say that I never saw braver men anywhere. Some of those who rushed up the hill will live in my memory forever." [5]

The retreating Spaniards took refuge in Santiago and held out for several days under land and sea bombardment. But on July 17 after the American forces had been reinforced, the Spanish flag was hauled down for the last time after 382 years.

The war was essentially over, although an American force was still to occupy Puerto Rico with little resistance. An armistice with Spain was signed on August 13. To the jingoists it was a "splendid little war," for the United States won the Philippines, Guam, and Puerto Rico, which now has a status somewhere between a colony and a state. But not, to the dismay of many, Cuba. Not quite.

Just before the United States had entered war it decided that it should demonstrate that its motives were not self-seeking by pledging not to annex Cuba. This was done by the Teller Amendment, named after the Colorado Senator who offered it. "That the United States hereby disclaims any disposition or intention to exercise sovereignty, jurisdiction, or control over the said island except for the pacification thereof, and asserts its determination, when that is accomplished, to leave the government and control of the island to its people." However, the self-denying character of the Teller Amendment was largely undone, as we shall soon see, by another amendment named after another senator.

But first we must take a brief look at another legacy of the Spanish–American War that was to have enduring consequences. For decades there had been feeling in the United States that it alone should build an isthmian canal despite the terms of the Clayton–Bulwer Treaty of 1850 that made it a joint British–American project. Now victorious America was unchallenged in the Western Hemisphere and it moved swiftly to remove the vexatious treaty. On January 11, 1899 Secretary of State John Hay and the British Ambassador, Lord Pauncefote, initialed a new treaty. It allowed the United States alone to build and operate a canal, although it must be open to all nations equally, even in time of war. But the treaty specifically prohibited fortification of the canal.

Teddy Roosevelt, now Governor of New York, and the expansionists immediately attacked the new treaty. He declared that "one prime reason for fortifying our great seaports is to unfetter our fleet, to release it for offensive purposes; and the proposed canal would fetter it again, for our fleet would have to watch it; and therefore do the work which a fort should do; and what it could do much better." [6] Roosevelt argued that it was contrary to the Monroe Doctrine for a non-American nation to have any say whatsoever about the canal. Both parties agreed with him and in their 1900 campaigns made that clear. And the Senate refused to ratify the first Hay–Pauncefote Treaty. Hay was prepared to resign but McKinley persuaded him to approach the British again. Britain, still isolated politically and needing American good will, had little choice but to go along. A second treaty, more by implication than specific language, gave the United States the right to acquire sovereignty over the site and fortify and defend a future canal.

While these crucial diplomatic and political decisions were being made, the United States was beginning its administration of the theoretically independent Cuba. Needless to say, the situation on the new island republic was chaotic. To its credit, the United States instituted numerous needed reforms: the cleaning of streets and sewers; the establishment of a sanitation system and a school system; the repair and construction of public works; a reorganization of the tax, court and university systems; the suppression of yellow fever in which pioneer work had been done by a Cuban physician, Carlos Finlay; and many more. Yet one fundamental fact was misunderstood by the military governor, General Leonard Wood, and many leading Americans. It is not surprising, for it is still misunderstood all over the world. Wood and the others overestimated the value of material progress. They did not recognize that most peoples would rather be poor under their own rule than somewhat better off under the rule of outsiders, however well motivated.

Although Cuba was nominally independent, it was in fact a dependency of the United States. No less an authority than General Wood himself said so:

> . . . Of course, the Platt Amendment has left Cuba with little or no independence . . . and the only course now is to seek annexation. . . . It cannot enter into certain treaties without our consent, nor seek loans beyond certain limits, and it must maintain the sanitary conditions established for it, all of which makes it very evident that it is entirely in our hands and I do not believe that a single European government would consider it other than what it is, a virtual dependency of the United States.[7]

General Wood's solution was, of course, that Cuba join the United States. This was not an unusual view, for all through American history there has been a strong feeling that the rest of the world progresses to the degree that it imitates the United States, and that the best thing that can happen to a foreign people is to be adopted and absorbed by this country. This is a genuine and well-meant belief, but it denies the possibility that other peoples might prefer their own way of life. And certainly this view has long antagonized others who cherish the values of their own cultures. Indeed, a major criticism of the United States over a period of decades has been that it has attempted to impose its values on much of the world. That this attempt is often well-meaning is seldom accepted as an excuse.

The Cubans wanted the freedom to govern their own land and that was denied them by the Platt Amendment. Since the Platt Amendment and the circumstances it fathered have been crucial not only to Cuban history but to American (one could argue that the Cuban missile crisis was a product of the Platt Amendment), it is necessary to examine it closely. Although drawn up by Secretary of War Elihu Root, it was named after the Senator who sponsored it, Orville H. Platt of Connecticut. Its most important provisions were these:

I. That the government of Cuba shall never enter into any treaty or other compact with any foreign power or powers which will impair or tend to impair the independence of Cuba, nor in any manner authorize or permit any foreign power or powers to obtain by colonization or for military or naval purposes or otherwise, lodgment in or control over any portion of said island. . . .

III. That the government of Cuba consents that the United States may exercise the right to intervene for the preservation of Cuban independence, the maintenance of a government adequate for the protection of life, property and individual liberty, and for discharging the obligations with respect to Cuba imposed by the Treaty of Paris on the United States, now to be assumed and undertaken by the government of Cuba. . . .

VII. That to enable the United States to maintain the independence of Cuba, and to protect the people thereof, as well as for its own defense, the government of Cuba will sell or lease to the United States lands necessary for coaling or naval stations at certain specified points to be agreed upon with the President of the United States.[8]

The United States insisted not only that the Platt Amendment be embedded in the Cuban constitution but in a *perpetual* treaty that could be modified only with the consent of both nations. The Cuban constitutional convention did not want to accept the Platt Amendment, for it was a clear infringement on their sovereignty. Nor did they want to surrender their sov-

ereign rights to territory to be used for American bases. There
was no way for American reassurances to disguise the fact that
Washington, not Havana, had the ultimate word in Cuban
affairs. But the Cubans accepted this language. They had no
choice, for the American Army was still in Cuba. Even when
the treaty was modified in 1934 under Franklin Delano Roosevelt, the United States retained the rights to the huge naval
base at Guantanamo Bay, a continuing source of friction between the neighboring states. We shall have frequent occasion,
in subsequent chapters, to return to Cuba, for it has been a
concern of just about every American president since the turn
of the century.

6
Dollar Diplomacy

Teddy Roosevelt is a dominant figure in American history and so must he be in these pages, for his actions in the first few years of the twentieth century established the character of American relations with Latin America for a third of a century, the era known, not quite accurately, as the era of Dollar Diplomacy. During those years the United States sent troops to five nations bordering on or in the Caribbean Sea. To understand why, it is necessary to know something about conditions in the area. Despite the passage of nearly three-quarters of a century, two world wars, a cold war, and millions of dollars of U.S. aid, conditions, except in Mexico, then were much as they are now.

The economy of most of Latin America had been developing along lines that have plagued it to this day. Each country was almost entirely dependent upon the export of one or two basic commodities: coffee, sugar, bananas, minerals, etc. Thus, the national economies became satellites of foreign economies, first Britain and then, in later decades, the United

States. They sold their commodities cheaply and purchased finished goods expensively. Because their economies were dominated by those of their industrial trading partners, they sold in a buyer's market and bought in a seller's market. This was not a problem for the great landowners who even at low prices made enormous sums, little of which had to go to the mass of the population which lived at a subsistence level.

Much of the problem stemmed from a holdover of the feudal tradition that land was the only way for a gentleman to make money. Commerce and industry were beneath them, so these vital components of a modern economy languished, a tendency encouraged by the industrial nations who profited most if Latin America—and Asia and Africa—served as suppliers of raw materials and purchasers of finished goods. These descendants of the Spanish and Portuguese took their own profits and reinvested them in more land or in American or European enterprises that were safer than investing at home.

The Latin American dictators who, with the backing of the landowners, largely governed the region—to the extent it was governed—welcomed foreign investors, who often paid handsome bribes to get concessions or franchises to build railroads or ports and to extract the nation's natural wealth. Not surprisingly, the foreign investers were more interested in stable conditions that would enable them to exploit local natural resources than they were in the welfare of the people. The politicians promised stability and to keep the plantation or mine workers in line in return for the foreign investors' support. It was an alliance that often meant that the officials of the foreign enterprises had as much or more authority than local government officials. And all too frequently government officials, local landowners, and resident foreign executives became members of a closely-knit society dedicated to profits for themselves.

Poverty among the masses was widespread and terrible. The gulf between the few rich and the many poor was so deep and wide that only small numbers, often ambitious soldiers, could cross. The masses of the people, Indian, black, or of mixed parentage, were exploited not only by the rich but by government officials at all levels.

It was the same throughout Latin America. There were "elected" presidents but the elections were often marked with fraud and coercion. There were political "parties" with distinctive names, usually Liberal and Conservative, but there was little to distinguish them, for they were usually just shifting alliances of factions seeking office and the power and wealth that went with it. There were noble constitutions, usually ignored, and courts, usually corrupt. There were armies, but they were little better than armed mobs, even though they were "the single most important factor in keeping a dictator or party in power. . . . They were almost random bands of ignorant, barefoot peasants usually drafted against their will, poorly trained if at all, and led by officers often corrupt and almost invariably untrained. Thus, even though the army was important, it was hardly more impressive than the bands recruited by revolutionaries. Further, army officers could often be bribed to join a revolution, bringing their ragtag soldiers with them." [1] Here, however, there is a difference nowadays. The armies are much better trained (the officers are often graduates of U.S. military schools) and better equipped (usually with U.S. equipment).

But basically there has been astonishingly little change. Frank Tannenbaum saw it this way:

The pattern of dictatorship and rebellion, followed by dictatorship, has not materially changed since 1900. Anyone who would make a count of the abortive uprisings and the successful rebellions in the last fifty years would convince himself that if matters have changed politically, the change has not necessarily been in the direction of greater stability. This is so in spite of an almost universal commitment to the ideals of democracy and constitutional government among Latin intellectuals and statesmen. . . . Obviously there is a gap between the democratic ideal aimed at by the reformers and the practical politics of actual government. . . . The social and cultural matrix within which Latin America's political leaders operate at present is such that effective and representative popular democracy is, with few exceptions, not a feasible alternative. The only really responsible question that a democratically-minded observer can ask of a politician in Latin America today is whether his conduct is conducive toward increasing the prospect of popular and representative government.[2]

In short, when Teddy Roosevelt took office after the assassination of McKinley (after a short time as governor of New York, Roosevelt became McKinley's running mate in the 1900 election), he found Latin America in something approaching chaos. His neighbors were certainly unruly but the question is: was it necessary for Roosevelt and his successors to try to establish order or would it have been better, for the United States and for Latin America, to leave them alone so they could settle their own affairs? But it may have been asking too much of the vigorous Roosevelt to stay out of the mess in the Caribbean, especially since he had his heart set on a canal across the isthmus.

Under Roosevelt the character of the Monroe Doctrine was to change significantly, although at first he seemed fairly complacent about European intervention in Latin America.

Shortly after taking office, Roosevelt in his annual message to Congress, on December 3, 1901, declared, "We do not guarantee any state against punishment if it misconducts itself, provided that punishment does not take the form of acquisition of territory by any non-American power." [3] This set the scene for a British-German-Italian armed intervention against Venezuela. The Venezuelan dictator, Cipriano Castro, was accused by the European powers of not permitting aliens to obtain justice in his courts. Britain and Germany, later joined by Italy, sent a naval expedition to Venezuela, lasting from December 1902 until March 1903. Several Venezuelan gunboats were sunk, several ports blockaded, and several forts bombarded. Castro quickly appealed to the United States for arbitration. Roosevelt urged the British and German ambassadors to settle the matter quickly because American public opinion was heating up. Castro came to terms with his European creditors, but then the question arose whether the three nations who had used force should have priority over those that had not. This question was sent to the Hague Permanent Court of Arbitration with the important result we shall soon examine.

Perhaps Roosevelt was not paying so much attention to the Venezuelan situation because he was in hot pursuit of one of his great dreams, an American canal that would enable the U.S. fleet and merchant marine to sail quickly back and forth from the Atlantic to the Pacific. He got his canal, but it is one of the less savory incidents in the history of U.S.–Latin American relations. As we saw earlier, the equipment of the French company that had attempted to build a canal was rusting in its works in Panama, then a part of Colombia. Speculators who had bought up at give-away prices the stock of the French company lobbied endlessly in Washington on behalf of the

Panama route, hoping to make a financial killing by selling to the United States the property, the equipment, and the little work accomplished. But the United States, after technical studies, had just about settled on a canal across Nicaragua. Although the canal itself would be longer, Nicaragua was considerably closer to both the Atlantic and Pacific coasts of the United States. Such a canal would also be cheaper because much work would be saved by connecting the canal to huge Lake Nicaragua. This would mean fewer locks, resulting both in lower construction costs and a more efficient canal.

A chief holder of stock in the old canal company was Philippe Bunau-Varilla, a Parisian who had been its chief engineer. He came to Washington and lobbied tirelessly among the senators and representatives. At the very last moment he got Congress to favor the Panamanian route. Roosevelt went along and persuaded his experts "to sanction the sudden change of sites . . . almost as if by sleight of hand." [4] The old company was paid $40 million and nobody has ever been able to find out whatever happened to the money, an enormous sum even now but an astronomical figure in those days.

The United States then negotiated a treaty with Colombia that would permit it to construct, fortify, and control the canal without affecting Colombia's sovereignty. For this Colombia was to receive $10 million in gold (compared with the $40 million the old company got) and an annual payment of $250,000. The United States promptly ratified the treaty but to Roosevelt's astonishment, and anger, Colombia did not. Its legislature did not want the old company to be able to sell its property without a big fee to the country, and it wanted more money from the United States. Whether or not this was a wise decision, it was one entirely within Colombia's right to make.

This did not mean that the canal was lost. Roosevelt could have patiently approached Colombia again and tried to work out a more acceptable deal or he could have returned to the original Nicaraguan route that was probably better anyway.

Roosevelt was not a patient man. Bunau-Varilla, who had worked such miracles of lobbying in Washington, now hurried down to Panama, where there had always been a certain amount of separatist sentiment. No one will be surprised that a rebellion soon broke out. Colombia sent a warship with 400 troops to put down the insurrection, but an American warship, the U.S.S. *Nashville*, acting on orders, blocked the Colombia force and the rebellion succeeded. The United States, normally slow to recognize revolutionary governments, recognized it immediately. Here it must be recalled that the United States had solemnly guaranteed Colombia's sovereignty in the Bidlack Treaty of 1846.

The versatile Buneau-Varilla again turned up in Washington, this time as Panama's emissary. He negotiated a treaty with the United States that he did not bother to show to the Panamanian authorities. Panama ratified it, nonetheless, because the treaty recognized Panama's independence. The treaty provided the same amount of money as the earlier one with Colombia, but in the most important aspect it was different. This one permitted the United States to act "as if it were sovereign" in the ten-mile-wide Canal Zone and also gave it the right to intervene in Panama itself if necessary to protect its independence. Panama, in effect, became an American colony, and this same treaty was to be the cause of anti-American riots sixty years later, in 1964.

Roosevelt never disclosed exactly what he did in 1903 but he did boast later that he "took the Canal Zone." And he was proud of it, writing to his friend Senator Henry Cabot Lodge in 1909, "The vital work, getting Panama as an independent republic, on which all else hinged, was done by me without the aid or advice of anyone, save in so far as they carried out my instructions; and without the knowledge of anyone." [5] The fact is simple. Roosevelt had seized territory from a nation whose sovereignty the United States had sworn to protect.

No sooner was this episode over than the Venezuelan affair reappeared. The Hague Court of Permanent Arbitration announced on February 22, 1904 that Britain, Germany, and Italy, the nations that had resorted to armed intervention, would have preference in the Venezuelan debt payments over those nations that had not intervened. Roosevelt worried about this. It seemed to foreshadow further armed interventions within the Monroe Doctrine area. From the President's concern came a declaration later termed the Roosevelt Corollary to the Monroe Doctrine. It became public in a letter that Roosevelt had his friend Elihu Root read at a New York dinner on May 20, 1904 celebrating the anniversary of Cuba's independence. These words are crucial to an understanding not only of American acts in Latin America in the first third of the century but, some might argue, to American policy the world over after World War II.

. . . It is not true that the United States has any land hunger or entertains any projects as regards other nations, save such as are for their welfare.

All that we desire is to see all neighboring countries stable, orderly, and prosperous. Any country whose people conduct themselves well can count upon our hearty friendliness. If a nation shows that it knows how to act with decency in industrial and political matters, if it keeps order and pays its obligations, then it need fear no interference from the United States. Brutal wrongdoing, or an impotence which results in a general loosening of the ties of civilized society, may finally require intervention by some civilized nation, and in the Western Hemisphere the United States cannot ignore this duty; but it remains true that our interests, and those of our southern neighbors, are in reality identical. All that we ask is that they shall govern themselves well, and be prosperous and orderly. Where this is the case they will find only helpfulness from us.[6]

By this declaration Roosevelt broadened the Monroe Doctrine to mean not only that others should keep hands off the Western Hemisphere but that the United States was no longer restricted to protection but could intervene as well. Critics of American foreign policy in Indochina have argued that the United States tends to think of itself as the world's policeman with the right to tell others how they should conduct their internal affairs. Roosevelt's declaration would seem to indicate that this is not a new tendency in American foreign policy.

This broader aspect aside, Roosevelt has had his defenders. Bemis, whose work is so essential to any study of U.S.–Latin American relations, argues that American interventions in the Dollar Diplomacy days were necessary to protect national security, that the United States could not risk foreign interventions in the vital Caribbean area. But it seems clear that by the early twentieth century the United States had no effective rivals in the Western Hemisphere, that no non-American state would have dared to challenge the Monroe Doctrine to the extent of permanent occupation of territory in Latin America, particularly in the Caribbean.

Roosevelt was worried about foreign investers getting justice in these chaotic lands. But these investers knew the risks they were taking, often made enormous profits, often exploited less-sophisticated Latin businessmen and governments, often bribed and cheated, and often unjustly appealed to their home government. The foremost American authority on Dollar Diplomacy, Dana G. Munro, saw it this way:

. . . It was often difficult to judge whether a given contract was so vitiated in its origin or so outrageous in its provisions as to make it unworthy of diplomatic support, because the evidence was apt to be unreliable and colored by partisan prejudice, and benefits obtained by the foreigner always had to be set off against the risks involved. Far too frequently, however, foreign governments supported claims without inquiring into the character and conduct of the claimants and without considering whether their demands might not be fraudulent or exaggerated. They tended to ignore considerations of fair play in their determination to teach the local authorities that they must respect their nationals simply because they were Germans, Italians, or Frenchmen.[7]

That is not to say that there were no injustices to foreign businessmen, but there are resorts other than force. All of these European countries had economic and diplomatic strength that the weak, impoverished Latin nations could hardly resist. And if the United States did feel it necessary to intervene, its economic, diplomatic, and political strength were such that the local governments would have had no choice but to submit. Nonetheless, an attempt must be made to see the problem in the context of the times. Armed intervention was still sanctioned by international law and custom. Powerful nations were accustomed to using their power, and there was certainly no tradition of sympathy for poor, unorganized societies. Indeed, just the contrary was true. The "civilized" nations had nothing but scorn for "banana republics," a feeling reinforced by convictions of racial superiority even more pronounced then than now. And it is true that Roosevelt and his immediate successors were concerned about the security of the Panama Canal and its approaches. It seems to be true that successive American interventions were dictated by a similar concern as much as for economic reasons. Thus, it seems fair to conclude that the term Dollar Diplomacy is not entirely fair.

Yet even attempting to see things in context, one can wonder why the United States concerned itself with the affairs of private investors who, after all, knew what they were getting into and often profited handsomely. Why should it have worried Washington if foreign nations did intervene militarily as long as those nations did not grab territory or establish naval bases? The United States had the diplomatic and military power to enforce its wishes in that respect. The answer seems to be that the United States intervened for the mixture of selfish and unselfish reasons that has usually characterized its Latin American policies. It genuinely wanted to help the people of these impoverished lands (invariably by attempting to impose American standards) and it was looking out for its own interests even if (as in Vietnam decades later) they were not really threatened.

The United States began edging into intervention in 1904 in the Dominican Republic. That unhappy land, torn alternately by revolutions and dictatorships, owed about $32 million to French, Belgian, German, Spanish, and Italian creditors. The situation was impossibly tangled, but finally in the fall of 1904 the United States, with Dominican agreement, began collecting customs revenue and paying a share to the foreign creditors.

The next step took place in Cuba, where the Platt Amendment gave the United States the right to intervene. Cuban politics were chaotic, with the always-present temptation for this or that faction to lure the United States into intervention on its side. This happened in 1906 when the first President, Tomás Estrada Palma, deliberately caused the government to collapse, feeling that American intervention would benefit him. Secretary of War William Howard Taft was in Cuba, sent there by Roosevelt to try to work out a political compromise. When Palma's government collapsed, Taft proclaimed himself, on September 29, as Provisional Governor of Cuba. Roosevelt was furious.

I am so angry with that infernal little Cuban republic that I would like to wipe its people off the face of the earth. All that we wanted from them was that they behave themselves and be prosperous and happy so that we would not have to interfere. And now, lo and behold, they have started an utterly pointless and unjustifiable revolution, and got things in such a snarl that we have no alternative but to intervene.[8]

Again, one can wonder if it would not have been better to stay out and let the Cubans settle things themselves. The intervention lasted more than two years and although it was the only armed intervention until the Bay of Pigs in 1961, it set the stage for a whole series of diplomatic, political, and economic interventions that caused the American ambassador often to be regarded as the most important man on the island. This established among some Cubans a legacy of distrust and anger that was a major factor in the split decades later between the new revolutionary government of Fidel Castro and the United States.

When Taft succeeded Roosevelt, he, too, was concerned with the Caribbean, but he put more emphasis on the economic aspects, believing that financial reform was the key to stability in that chronically unstable area. He soon got involved with Nicaragua, whose dictator, José Santos Zelaya, was trying to take power in neighboring countries. Two Americans were involved in a revolution against Zelaya. When they were captured by his forces and shot, the United States actively began to assist the dictator's enemies. The situation was complicated almost beyond belief.

Eventually Zelaya resigned, only to be followed by a succession of squabbling and ineffective leaders, with rebellion after rebellion. The United States involved itself intimately with events, backing this leader and opposing that. Finally, when the situation was in complete chaos, the American minister, in early August 1912, called ashore one hundred sailors from the U.S.S. *Annapolis* to guard the legation. Soon marines were landed and reinforcements sent from the United States. A few Americans were killed and many Nicaraguans. By October the military situation was in hand and most of the American troops left. One hundred marines remained, a symbol of United States determination to regulate Nicaraguan affairs and, more important, a symbol all through Latin America of North American imperialism.

Nicaragua's finances were turned over to Wall Street bankers, thus lending credence to the slogan, Dollar Diplomacy. And the marines, as scholar Dexter Perkins has written, kept "in power an unpopular regime." And Dana G. Munro wrote:

In Nicaragua, the continued presence of the legation guard was interpreted to mean that no revolution would be tolerated. This meant that the conservatives would stay in power, though everyone, including the State Department, knew they were a minority party. The arguments advanced in defense of this policy: the assertion that the liberals included a large proportion of the "ignorant mob," and that most of their leaders represented the evil *zelayista* tradition, were perhaps put forward in all sincerity by officials who had little contact with any except the conservatives, but they made little sense to anyone who had friends in both parties. The support of a minority government was inconsistent with the principles that govern American policy in the Caribbean, but for more than ten years no Secretary of State wanted to assume responsibility for the revolution that would almost certainly follow the legation guard's withdrawal.[9]

In 1925, the United States decided to risk withdrawing its small contingent. Thirteen years of American intervention had made little difference. A revolution erupted almost immediately and soon the marines were sent back. They remained until January 1933.

The only way to judge this, and the other interventions, is to examine their results. The United States had accomplished the supervising of elections (which always returned friendly candidates), had trained a national constabulary, and kept Nicaragua's tangled finances in reasonable shape. But what were the long-term results? A few years after the marines left, the head of the National Guard, General Anastasio Somoza, established a brutal and repressive regime that has kept his family in power, and provided them with great riches, to this day. Not a noble end to the well-intentioned U.S. intervention. Again one must ask: might not the people of Nicaragua have been better off if the United States had left them alone?

7
President Wilson Intervenes

No president has been more closely identified in the American mind with peace and democracy than Woodrow Wilson. Yet the fact is that he ordered American troops into three Latin countries: Mexico in 1914, Haiti in 1915, and the Dominican Republic in 1916. Although the Mexican intervention was brief, it illustrated the difficulty of applying moral judgments to the internal affairs of other countries.

Mexico was the only Latin country other than Cuba where Americans had made massive investments. Foreigners had more than half the investments in Mexico and more than half the foreign investments were American. Also some 40,000 Americans lived in Mexico. Thus, as is usually the case, the United States favored stability in Mexico so that Americans and their investments would be safe. This stability was provided by a more or less benevolent dictator, Porfirio Díaz, whose iron-handed rule had begun in 1876. But the appearance of stability was deceptive; beneath the surface the forces of social revolution were at work, a condition that today exists in most of Latin America.

These forces erupted in 1910–1911 in the first great social revolution in Latin American history. Over a period of years the revolution sharply curtailed the power of the Roman Catholic Church in Mexico, redistributed much of the land of the great landowners, improved the lot of the Indians in such areas as education and health, and greatly broadened the base of political power. A decent and honorable man, Francisco I. Madero, became President of Mexico but he was not able to control the terrible turbulence set free by revolution. He was ousted by one of his own generals, Victoriano Huerta, who pledged his personal honor to the safety of Madero. A few days later Madero and his Vice-President were shot, attempting to escape, or so Huerta claimed. This happened in early 1913 when Taft had only a few days left in office. The American public was so outraged by the death of the two Mexican statesmen that Taft decided to leave the question of recognition of the Huerta government to Wilson.

Wilson's advisers recommended that he recognize the Huerta government on the old diplomatic principle that recognition did not imply approval, merely the recognition that the government had effective power. But Wilson, with his profound moral sense, decided that recognition would be immoral. At first this may seem a just decision, but even the most moral man has difficulty in making moral judgments about another society, particularly in a revolutionary situation. How is a foreigner to judge the morality of another government and, even more difficult, how does he judge the will of the people in an alien society?

Bemis examined this difficult question.

Right here, when he searches for the will of the people outside his own land, the Wilsonian is overwhelmed, or certain ultimately to be overwhelmed, by a tangle of difficulties in applying his policy of judgment on revolutions against other constitutions than his own. In many Latin American countries, not to mention the rest of the world, governments have been republican only in form and letter. Once ensconced in constitutional authority, a government, that is to say a strong man, by control of electoral machinery, the police and the army, can extend his power under color of the constitution.

To deny the right of revolution against such a regime would be to frustrate real self-government. Wilson's answer to this . . . presumably would have been that the revolutionary government might be recognized if sanctioned by the will of the people. But what is the will of the people . . . ? At best the tasks and responsibilities of sitting in judgment on revolutions, even if judgment could be politically unbiased, extend to infinite gradations, degrees, circumstances, difficulties, diplomacies, and inconsistencies. That is why traditional international practice has avoided the danger of dogma dealing with this problem. . . .[1]

(Although it is remote from Latin America, this question of recognition had even greater consequence in 1949 when Harry S. Truman refused to recognize the Mao Tse-tung government in China, initiating a period of tension between the two great nations that has had a profound influence on postwar history, being perhaps even the basic cause of the Vietnam War.)

Wilson was not content to refuse recognition of the Huerta government; he decided to unseat the dictator. First he secretly allowed Huerta's opponents to obtain arms in the United States. Then on Feburary 3, 1914, he openly ended the arms embargo, encouraging Huerta's foes and enraging him. As tensions grew, an incident in Tampico moved the United

States closer to open intervention. In early April a party of American sailors went ashore to buy supplies for the U.S.S. *Dolphin.* A Mexican junior officer ordered their seizure and paraded them through the streets. The American naval commander demanded their release, which was immediately ordered by a senior Mexican officer who also extended his nation's regrets. Huerta himself apologized as well. This was not enough for the United States, and the naval commander, with Wilson's backing, demanded a twenty-one gun salute to the American flag. Huerta refused and tensions increased further.

Wilson then, on April 20, asked Congress to authorize the use of armed force to obtain respect for the United States. But a day later, a day before he got the authorization, he ordered the Navy to seize the port of Vera Cruz, to prevent the landing of arms arriving on a German freighter. Several Mexicans were killed and Wilson found himself in control of the territory of a sovereign state. He didn't want to stay, but he didn't want to leave either as long as Huerta was in power. Fortunately, Argentina, Brazil, and Chile offered themselves as joint mediators. Wilson gratefully accepted and so did Huerta, who soon resigned and fled into exile in which eventually he died a poor man. But the removal of the odious Huerta did not improve things in Mexico much. U.S. troops left Vera Cruz on November 23, 1914, but Mexico became a chaotic battlefield for the revolutionary forces of such legendary leaders as Carranza, Villa, and Zapata.

The United States, together with a group of Latin states, decided to settle on Venustiano Carranza. This enraged Pancho Villa, who made a series of daring, and bloody, raids across the border into the United States. Wilson ordered General John J. Pershing to pursue Villa and punish him. Carranza could not permit Villa to become a hero, so he demanded that the United States leave Mexico immediately. It was now early 1917, war with Germany was impending, and Wilson wanted to end his aggravating involvement. So he called Pershing back, and when the Mexican Congress formally made Carranza President and adopted a liberal constitution, Wilson thought he could call it quits. He did and the Mexican problem quickly faded away. Wilson's Mexican policy could hardly be termed a triumph. Even the sympathetic Bemis saw it this way:

. . . He intervened diplomatically to save the Mexican people from a new dictator. This novel action, the product of idealism and inexperience, involved him against his will in limited military interventions, and it very nearly brought the United States into an unnecessary war with Mexico at an extraordinarily critical moment of its history. He opened full wide the sluiceways of a revolution that distressed and ravaged the people beyond measure. Hundreds of American citizens lost their lives in the ensuing violence. Most of the survivors left the country, abandoning their homes and property. In subsequent decades, hundreds of millions of legitimately invested American capital was lost. Destruction of the property of the Mexican *cientificos* naturally turned against the United States the survivors of that elite, the most intelligent and able fraction of the population. The interventions in the port of Vera Cruz and the northern states alienated the remainder. For a long time afterward neither the suffering people of Mexico nor their successive governments were sincere friends of the United States.[2]

Wilson's Latin American policy was much like Teddy Roosevelt's: if any of those unruly nations misbehaved, the United States would carry out its obligations to civilization and spank them. Not long after the Mexican affair Wilson concluded that he had to spank Haiti and the Dominican Republic, those chaotic neighbors who shared the Caribbean island of Hispaniola.

Haiti came first. It was one of the few French colonies in Latin America. There, on the western third of Hispaniola, a few white planters and French officials ruled hundreds of thousands of African slaves. After the French Revolution, a slave rebellion broke out in 1791. The slaves in their overwhelming numbers all but exterminated the whites, and independence was proclaimed in 1804. A feeble sort of government was maintained in Port-au-Prince by mulattoes who considered and called themselves the elite. They spoke French, practiced Catholicism, maintained a French culture and sometimes sent their children to Paris to study. But the bulk of the population was made up of black peasants who spoke a *patois*, a mixture of French and African languages, practiced *voodoo*, that mysterious religion that is still widely followed in the countryside. There was always tension betwen the mulattoes of the city and the blacks of the countryside, but neither faction could rule without some support from the other. As was the case with their Spanish-speaking neighbors, Haiti was ruled by a succession of dictators.

Shortly after Wilson took office, the President of Haiti, Tancrède Auguste, died suddenly. His funeral procession was interrupted by the gunfire of rival forces. Rival succeeded rival, and even by Caribbean standards the chaos was unimaginable. Haiti's finances collapsed and foreign creditors set up a clamor. Wilson suggested that Haiti might want the United States to administer its customs. Successive presidents turned down the idea and life in Port-au-Prince became a nightmare. On March 4, 1915, General Vilbrun Guillaume Sam was elected President, the third in six months. Another revolution erupted and the details are uncertain. Sam sought refuge in the French Legation but reportedly left orders for political prisoners to be executed. Some 170 were killed, many of them members of the elite. Their relatives went on a rampage. They invaded the French Legation, dragged Sam out from under a bed and tore him to pieces in the street.

As this was happening, the U.S.S. *Washington* sailed into the harbor and Admiral Caperton, acting on instructions, restored order and took charge of the city. A new President was elected, and by fall he had agreed to a treaty that gave the United States complete control of the country. Many Haitians accepted protectorate status without much hostility, particularly the elite. One of their group was now President and the Americans would keep the men of the countryside, the *cacos*, out of the capital. And U.S. economic aid would be welcome. But there were other Haitians who wanted to run their own country and in the interior many took up arms. There was heavy fighting in September and October; then Washington, alarmed by reports of heavy Haitian casualties, ordered Caperton to end offensive operations. By February 1916 most of the armed bands had been dispersed and the Haitian constabulary, led by marine officers and sergeants, had effective control of the country.

Unlike Nicaragua, where the American Legation guard merely guaranteed the rule of friendly officials, in Haiti American direction went down several levels into the various government departments. Thus white Americans were the conspicuous rulers of a black nation. And this rule was not as effective as it might have been since authority was divided between the State and Navy Departments. Nonetheless, there were solid accomplishments in the fields of public works, health, finance, and agriculture, and the Garde d'Haiti was well organized under the direct command of a marine officer. There was little progress, however, in fostering the spirit of democracy, perhaps because there was almost no progress in establishing a school system. Most Haitians were illiterate when the Americans arrived in 1915 and most were still illiterate when the Yankees left nineteen years later.

As the years went on, relations between Haitians and the Americans began to deteriorate. One reason was racial. Soon after the wives of American officials began to arrive, racial tensions began to develop. Further, Haitians began to get impatient to see their uninvited guests leave. An armed insurrection erupted in March 1919 and lasted more than a year. Some 2,000 Haitians were killed, "brigands," according to the Americans, "patriots," to most Haitians. During the fighting there were frequent reports of American atrocities. These shocked U.S. public opinion and caused a couple of inquiries which found that most of the charges could not be substantiated. These reports nonetheless damaged the United States throughout Latin America. Violence erupted again in 1929 and President Herbert Hoover decided that the U.S. occupation should end as soon as possible. Nonetheless, it took another five years before the United States withdrew.

For some years after that it seemed that the American occupation had enabled Haiti to find stable government. The first few presidents ruled well, although it soon became apparent that the real force in the country was the Garde d'Haiti, the American-trained constabulary. Eventually the inherent weaknesses of Haitian society reasserted themselves and in the first eight months of 1957 there were seven governments. Finally, following a questionable election, a physician, François (Papa Doc) Duvalier, became President. For thirteen years, until he died in early 1971, Papa Doc kept himself in power by methods brutal even by Caribbean standards, but he did little to improve the desperate lot of his people. For much of that time he was supported by the United States, perhaps because there seemed no alternative. He was succeeded by a young son and it is, at the time of this writing, too soon to say what will happen in poor, unfortunate Haiti. So again, despite some real achievements, it is difficult to see any long-term benefits to the country from American intervention.

The most significant of Wilson's three interventions was in the Dominican Republic because from it stemmed the much more spectacular American intervention in 1965, one that sparked a world-wide controversy. The customs receivership in the Dominican Republic established by Teddy Roosevelt had provided some benefit but hardly enough to overcome the basic problems of that improverished island republic. Serious troubles began when the able Ramón Cáceres was assassinated in November 1911. His Cabinet was not able to maintain control and by early 1912, bands of insurgents were roaming the country. President Taft became alarmed and in September sent 750 marines to Santo Domingo. They remained aboard ship but their mere presence allowed the United States to call the turns. The United States forced one president out of office and in November the Archbishop of Santo Domingo, Monsignor Adolfo Nouel, was elected by congress as Provisional President. The marines pulled out, but shortly afterward the Archbishop became sick. He tried to resign but the American minister persuaded him to hold off.

As soon as Wilson took office in Washington, he was confronted by the deteriorating situation in the Dominican Republic. He immediately cabled the Archbishop, asking him to stay on, but the clergyman soon embarked on a ship to Europe. Now Wilson was concerned not only with the situation in Mexico and Haiti and with the war in Europe but the situation in Santo Domingo seemed on the verge of collapse. A new Provisional President was elected, José Bordas Valdéz. The United States then supervised the election of a constituent assembly which was dominated by Bordas' political foes. It soon became apparent that Bordas wanted to become the regular President. He made preparations to control the presidential elections, but before they could be held, in April 1914, a revolution broke out.

The United States sought desperately for some sort of compromise. When none appeared possible Washington informed Santo Domingo that the contending factions must choose a Provisional President. He was to hold elections. If they were fair, the United States would support the new government and not permit further revolution. If the elections were not fair, the United States would order another. That was that—period. And to back up the ultimatum, another contingent of marines was sent, but again they stayed aboard ship.

The elections were held in October 1914, with two Americans at each polling place. Juan Isidro Jiménez, an old-time politician, won narrowly over another veteran politician. He was barely in office when the United States told him it wanted additional powers. He refused, backed by his Congress. But Jiménez, elderly and in ill health, could not control the contending leaders and there was dissension in the government. Amidst growing hostility between the Dominican leaders and the United States, Washington demanded a treaty that would give the United States the same right to intervene that it had in Cuba. Jiménez was horrified and sent a personal letter to Wilson saying that his government would be jeopardized if word of the demand became public. Washington now told Jiménez that it was going to appoint a financial adviser with very wide powers and a director of a much-expanded constabulary. He turned this down.

By January 1916 the American minister feared another revolution and he was instructed to tell Jiménez that the United States would send troops to put down any rebellion. This was not much help to him, for he knew that any government kept in power by U.S. troops would lose all popular support. Finally in May the old man, exhausted and beset by his political foes on one side and by the United States on the other, resigned.

His successor was no more eager to give in to U.S. demands. The withholding of funds by the United States was not successful in getting cooperation; it succeeded only in causing the Americans to be blamed for the deteriorating economic situation. The people were getting restive and things threatened to get out of hand in October when U.S. marines, attempting to arrest a local leader, got into a gun battle in which a marine captain and a sergeant were killed. The next day a marine patrol was attacked and three Dominicans were killed in the fight. Washington saw no way out except a full-scale military occupation. Wilson gave his approval on November 26, 1916.

While the American control in Haiti had been complete, the country was at least permitted a nominal government. When the provisional government in the Dominican Republic said it would consider staying in office to help, the U.S. Military Governor said the ministers could suit themselves but that they would get no recognition and no salary. Naval officers then took over at every level of government to the humiliation of local officials. And the Dominican Congress was suspended.

Again, as in Nicaragua and Haiti, there was armed resistance. Again the resisters were called "bandits" by the Americans and again there were reports of atrocities. A Congressional investigation later uncovered grave abuses by the U.S. occupation forces. Yet although there was much to criticize about the American occupation, there were also substantial accomplishments in public works, public health, and, most important, in education. Student enrollment was raised in eight years from 12,000 to more than 100,000.

Hostility toward the Americans, always present, began to increase in 1919 and growing criticism of the United States, at home and abroad, caused the State Department to be eager to end the occupation. But the Navy insisted that it needed much more time for necessary reforms. Finally in 1924, after Horacio Vásquez was elected in elections supervised by the United States, the marines pulled out.

As in Haiti, it seemed at first that the U.S. occupation had established momentum that would mean lasting stability. But Vásquez could not resist seeking the re-election that was barred by the Dominican constitution. As usual a revolution broke out and as in Nicaragua and Haiti, the American-trained constabularly was the dominant force. Its leader was Rafael Leonidas Trujillo Molina. There have been many tyrants in Latin American history, but it is difficult to think of one whose name has become as infamous as Trujillo's. He brought a certain measure of prosperity and stability to his country, but the Dominican people paid a terrible price in repression and brutality and corruption unsurpassed in modern history. Trujillo and his family took for themselves a vast fortune, estimated in the hundreds of millions of dollars. He did not hesitate to spend lavishly—in entertainment and bribes—to protect himself. He knew that the support, or at least the indulgence, of the American government was essential. He invited scores of prominent Americans to his country, among them Senators and Representatives, entertained them richly, and most of them returned to the United States praising the despot as a great man. For three decades he filled his jails with political opponents. They were the lucky ones, for it is widely believed that his agents murdered political foes in Mexico, Puerto Rico, even the United States, and, of course, at home. He was finally assassinated in May 1961, and the turmoil, violence, and death that followed three decades of tyranny have persisted to this day in the Dominican Republic. Any judgment of the first U.S. intervention must take this into account.

So, too, is it necessary to consider these interventions in any judgment of Woodrow Wilson. As a foremost Wilson scholar, Arthur S. Link has written, "There is a certain irony in this whole story. The man who . . . abhorred the very thought of using force in international relations became the first president in the history of the United States to use violence in imposing its will on nations which were, at least theoretically, free and sovereign." [3]

Before leaving the era of Dollar Diplomacy it is necessary to examine briefly the continued determination of the Latin American nations to bring the United States to the principle of nonintervention. During these years, particularly in the 1920s and early 1930s, there was an increasing number of Pan-American conferences in which this country pushed for closer Pan-American relations including the United States,

and in which the Latin nations untiringly pushed nonintervention. The United States, of course, argued that a Pan-
American movement would benefit the entire Western Hemisphere. But there were Latin Americans who took a strongly
opposite view. One such was José Ingenieros of Argentina, a
psychologist and sociologist. He declared in Buenos Aires in
October 1922:

We are not, we no longer wish to be, we could not continue to be
Pan-Americanists. . . . If the Monroe Doctrine might conceivably
have been a guarantee during the past century of the "principle of
nationalities" against the "right of intervention," it is evident today
that that Doctrine . . . sets forth the "right of intervention" of the
United States as against the Latin–American "principle of nationalities." A hypothetical guarantee was turned into a present danger.
. . . That equivocal Doctrine, which never managed to be applied
against European interventions, has had the function, finally, of as-
suring the exclusiveness of United States interventions. . . . This is
what recent United States imperialist policy which has followed an
alarming course for all Latin America, suggests to us.[4]

An American, and somewhat different view, was expressed
by the *Chicago Tribune* in 1922.

. . . We do not wish to anticipate the future, but everything leads us
to surmise that sooner or later Mexico will bow to our sovereignty. If
we cared to be prophetic, we would say that the nations to the south
will feel our attraction by virtue of the law of political gravity. Penetration and absorption could be gradual or union might be born out
of a crisis. A country like Mexico cannot remain in a state of economic stagnation and of social and political chaos.[5]

In 1923 at the fifth Pan-American Conference at Santiago
de Chile, Professor Alejandro Álvarez of the host delegation,
argued that the Latin American nations even before reaching

formal agreement had subscribed to certain principles different from the international law observed in Europe. He cited as an example "nonintervention and the non-occupation of territories of the States of America by ultra-continental countries." [6] Yet this was still short of nonintervention by American states as well. By 1925, however, the Governing Board of the Pan American Union had received a proposal that "no Nation has a right to interfere in the internal or foreign affairs of an American Republic against the will of that Republic. . . ." [7] It is significant that this was forwarded to the Pan American Union by Charles Evans Hughes, one of the nation's foremost attorneys, then Secretary of State and later Chief Justice of the United States. Significant, too, is the fact that he evidently did not first submit the proposal to State Department legal experts. They, no doubt, would have opposed it.

By 1925 Frank B. Kellogg had succeeded Hughes as Secretary of State. He was a keen supporter of the International Court of Justice, so he slowed down those Americans who advocated the development of a peculiarly American international law. In 1927 the Commission of Jurists meeting at Rio de Janeiro again pushed for the adoption of the doctrine of nonintervention. The State Department did not like the idea much.

In 1928 there was the famous Kellogg–Briand Pact that was supposed to end war for all time. Signed in Paris on August 27, the parties to it renounced war and agreed that all disputes would be settled by pacific means. Immediately it was asked: did this mean that the United States had renounced the Roosevelt Corollary to the Monroe Doctrine by which it had felt empowered to intervene in the internal affairs of Latin states? The State Department undertook a study that seemed to mean the end of the Roosevelt Corollary. On December 17, 1928, a memorandum from Under Secretary J. Reuben Clark, Jr. concluded that "it is not believed that this corollary is justified by the terms of the Monroe Doctrine, however much it may be justified by the application of the law of self-preservation." [8]

Thus, another step was taken toward the doctrine of nonintervention. More significant, however, was an article written during the 1928 campaign in which Teddy Roosevelt's cousin, Franklin Delano Roosevelt, criticized American intervention. He called on the United States to renounce "for all time" the practice of "arbitrary intervention in the home affairs of our neighbors," thus foreshadowing the Good Neighbor Policy that followed his election as President four years later.

But there were other developments during that year of 1928 that demonstrated continued U.S. opposition to nonintervention. The sixth Pan-American Conference was held in Havana. The United States was so conscious of its importance that President Calvin Coolidge addressed it. Again the Latin nations pushed for an absolute rule of nonintervention. Again the United States was not yet willing to abandon the protection of its citizens against a denial of justice or to give up the right of intervention when a nation refused to arbitrate a dispute involving such a denial. Charles Evans Hughes succeeded in blocking a nonintervention article and defended the continuing interventions in Nicaragua and Haiti as temporary. The question was postponed for further discussion at the seventh Pan-American Conference.

In 1930 Henry L. Stimson was Hoover's Secretary of State. An old comrade of Teddy Roosevelt and a firm supporter of the Rough Rider's corollary, it was now his duty to declare that "the Monroe Doctrine was a declaration of the United States versus Europe—not of the United States versus Latin America." And his Undersecretary, William R. Castle, Jr. asserted that the Monroe Doctrine "conferred no superior position on the United States." [9] But the full adoption by the United States of the principle of nonintervention was still some years off.

8
The Years of
the Good Neighbor

The year 1932 saw the election, in the midst of a terrible depression, of Franklin Delano Roosevelt as President of the United States. Clearly, his overwhelming preoccupation had to be the economic recovery of the country. Thus, his inaugural address concentrated on domestic problems. He did, however, use a term that came to characterize the policy of his successive administrations toward Latin America. He declared that it would be the policy of his administration to be a good neighbor in the world. Although he was then speaking of the world as a whole, the term Good Neighbor Policy soon came to apply specifically to Latin America, no doubt because the new president devoted a great deal of sympathetic attention to the area. He made plans for the withdrawal of U.S. troops from Haiti, tried to avoid substantial involvement in the chronically tangled affairs of Cuba, indicated a willingness to negotiate substantial modifications of the Platt Amendment that gave the United States the right to intervene in Cuba, and in general radiated a greater friendliness toward Latin

America than that region had ever before seen in an American president.

The Good Neighbor Policy has been described as being primarily "one of spirit. It cost nothing in dollars or material aid. Its essence was to give up rights of intervention, tutelage, and —up to a point—even leadership. The beauty of it, from Washington's point of view, lay in its negative quality. To desist from doing things that we had done was relatively easy. There was an element of risk, and specific American interests sometimes suffered, but on balance the policy paid off handsomely." [1]

Another view was that "despite its immediate success, it is difficult to perceive enduring contributions of the policy to inter-American relations or to conditions in the hemispheric republics." [2] An even less enthusiastic view is that of the Mexican historian, Alonso Aguilar.

Of course, the Good Neighbor Policy was not precisely what many people desired or supposed it to be—the end of imperialism—but neither was it an empty phrase. It was a step forward as far as the aggressive behavior of the United States was concerned, behavior which had culminated in armed interventions in Mexico, Central America, and the Caribbean. It also constituted a victory for the democratic forces of the continent.

Roosevelt's policy did not succeed in modifying the monopolistic structure of the United States economy, nor in a deeper sense, did it seek to do so. Neither did it affect the very basis of United States-Latin American relations. The countries south of the Rio Grande remained subjugated to the great power in the north and very soon the illusion vanished that things would change radically. [3]

It seems to be true that things did not change as much as some hoped but there were substantial reasons. First, the United States and most of the world were in a terrible depression. Then along came World War II and almost immediately after it, the Cold War. The trend started by Roosevelt never really had the opportunity to develop but, nonetheless, an important beginning had been made.

In 1933 the seventh Pan-American Conference was held at Montevideo, Uruguay. The American delegation was headed by Secretary of State Cordell Hull, who went to great lengths to be cooperative. At Montevideo a nonintervention proposal was adopted by the body for the first time. "No state has the right to intervene in the internal or external affairs of another." The United States went along—but not quite the whole way. Hull declared that the United States reserved its rights by "the law of nations as generally recognized." There was still a holding back.

Shortly after Montevideo, Roosevelt made a series of declarations that defined his view of nonintervention. He asserted that only singlehanded interventions were improper. He said that if law and order broke down, it might be necessary for the other hemispheric nations to participate in a joint intervention. But this raised then, and still does, an immediate objection. Could not a joint intervention really mean a disguised American intervention with the United States using its domination of the Pan-American system to obtain authorization for such a move? This, of course, has been the basis for the objection of many Latin Americans to the whole idea of the Pan-American movement. They have argued for decades that Pan-Americanism merely provides the sheep's clothing for the North American wolf.

Nonetheless, most informed Latin Americans welcomed any movement toward the principle of nonintervention, as they did the series of steps taken by Roosevelt in succeeding months. The United States divested itself of its rights to intervene in

Cuba, Panama, Haiti, and the Dominican Republic. Most important was the voluntary surrender in 1934 of the intervention rights in Cuba conferred by the Platt Amendment. The United States, however, still had almost decisive influence over Cuba. By 1933 Americans had invested about a billion dollars in Cuba, almost half of it in sugar. Since sugar dominated the economy of Cuba, the island was an economic, if not political, colony of the United States.

It was in 1933 in Cuba that chaotic events unfolded swiftly with a result that was to influence the Cuban–American break of 1960–1961 and contribute to the Bay of Pigs and Cuban missile crises of the Kennedy administration. The President of Cuba was Gerardo Machado, friendly to the United States but a terrible despot at home, with murder and violence as his most effective instruments to remain in power. As revolutionary fervor against Machado grew, Roosevelt sent to Cuba as ambassador Assistant Secretary Sumner Welles, the most prestigious Latin American expert in the State Department and a trusted personal adviser. In September he forced Machado's resignation, and amidst confusion a group of army sergeants rebelled. One of them, Fulgencio Batista, took charge. The revolution quickly spread. The sergeants were joined by university students, some professors, and some political radicals. Amidst the normal confusion of these circumstances, Professor Ramón Grau San Martín became the leader and soon headed the government. As reported by Hugh Thomas in his monumental *Cuba: The Pursuit of Freedom*, Cubans felt that "for the first time Cuba had 'an authentically revolutionary government backed and nourished by the great popular masses without the previous authorization of Washington and its agent in Cuba.' " [4]

Although that may have overstated the depth and breadth

of Grau's support, there is little doubt that he was the effective head of the Cuban government. Spain and a handful of Latin American governments recognized him quickly, but the rest of Latin America and the world waited to see what Roosevelt would do. In those days, while the Platt Amendment was still in effect, American recognition was absolutely vital for a Cuban government. Welles, despite his Latin American experience, began to get rattled. He thought he smelled the odor of Communism around Grau, a foreshadowing of later Cuban crises. Welles counseled intervention and American ships were sent to patrol the coast. Other advisers, however, informed Roosevelt that Welles's view of Communist strength was exaggerated.

Welles specifically recommended that Grau's government not be recognized because it was not sufficiently stable, yet it was the failure of Washington to recognize Grau that prevented his consolidating power. Welles was confident that no Cuban government could long survive without American recognition. He was right. Although Grau hung on for several months, when it became obvious that he would never get U.S. recognition, he resigned, on January 16, 1934. Batista, by now leader of the Cuban army, now had unchallenged power and he appointed Colonel Carlos Mendieta as President. Mendieta took the oath of office on January 18, and on January 23 his government was recognized by Washington.

This experience reinforced Roosevelt's instinctive distaste for intervention and he quickly moved to negotiate with the new government a treaty abrogating the intervention rights of the Platt Amendment. The treaty was signed on May 29 and ratified by the Senate two days later. But to many Cuban nationalists, it was too late. The United States had already intervened to block the choice of the revolution. The question was not the fitness of Grau to govern. Indeed, he proved later to be a bad leader. The question was whether or not the Cubans had the right to choose their own leader, good or bad. This was to rankle Cubans for years, and Fidel Castro decades later was to cite the Grau–Welles affair as a basic grievance. For not only did Welles block Grau but the collapse of the Grau government put Batista in power and the former sergeant was to become a tyrant, yet one welcomed, until almost the very end, by a succession of American presidents.

The year 1936 saw historic developments in those two areas that have dominated U.S.–Latin American relations: Pan-Americanism and the doctrine of nonintervention. Americans have long favored the Pan-American movement. Outside the government the primary motive has been no doubt a real, although romantic, belief in the community of interests of the peoples of the Western Hemisphere, despite the fact that the Hispanic heritage of Latin America is far different from the Anglo-Saxon and European heritage of the United States. Indeed, it seems inarguable that America's cultural affinities go east to Great Britain and Europe rather than south to Latin America. Within the government, however, the basic impetus toward Pan-Americanism has been clear: it provides the most effective, and least offensive, way for the United States to exert leadership over the entire hemisphere. Sensitive spirits are less easly bruised if the United States consults with its neighbors to receive cooperation rather than demanding it.

Conversely, the Latin nations have had little alternative to recognizing the leadership of the United States. Indeed, they often welcome it. There is also a great deal of genuine admiration for American achievements and the inevitable hope that the United States will help its much poorer neighbors. But the Colossus of the North inevitably has inspired fear as well as admiration, a fear which is based not only on power but on history.

These two great themes—Pan-Americanism and nonintervention—intersected at the Pan-American Conference in Buenos Aires, Argentina, in December 1936. It was an extraordinary occasion. President Roosevelt, fresh from his landslide re-election victory, arrived in Argentina aboard a battleship. He was given a wild reception, attended the first session, and then departed as he came, leaving the work of the conference to Cordell Hull and the other foreign ministers. On December 23, 1936, the participants in the conference signed a treaty for "the Maintenance, Preservation, and Reestablishment of Peace" that stipulated mutual consultation, without specifying how, "in the event of war or a virtual state of war between the American states." [5] However, the Pan-Americanization of foreign relations dealt primarily with conflicts within the hemisphere.

Of much greater significance was the success, finally, of the Latin nations in gaining American acceptance, in binding language, of the principle of nonintervention. This was embodied in the Additional Protocol Relative to Non-Intervention. These words are from its most important article:

Article I. The High Contracting Parties declared inadmissible the intervention of any one of them, directly or indirectly, and for whatever reason, in the internal and external affairs of any other of the Parties. . . .[6]

Secretary of State Hull was among those signing the Protocol which was later ratified by the Senate without reservation and without a dissenting vote. Over a period of time the Protocol was ratified by enough other signatories to make it a binding treaty. At last it seemed that the United States could no longer intervene south of the Rio Grande. There was one semantic difficulty, however. The Protocol prohibited intervention by "any one" of the signatories. It has never been made clear whether this meant a joint intervention was possible. But in any case the United States was prohibited from a unilateral intervention. It seemed as if the days of American intervention were over forever, particularly when the principle of nonintervention was later embodied in the Charter of the United Nations and of the Organization of American States. But, as we shall see, the United States was to intervene unilaterally in Guatemala in 1954, in Cuba in 1961, and in the Dominican Republic in 1965.

In the mid-1930s and early 1940s a Latin American fad developed in the United States and for a while, such is the fashion in this fad-vulnerable nation, seemed irresistible. Latin American music was sung and danced everywhere, pop composers turned out by the score such songs as "Mexicali Rose" and "South of the Border"; such Latin performers as Carmen Miranda and Desi Arnaz became big stars; clothing, jewelry, and home decoration fashions were greatly influenced by the colors and designs of Latin American Indians. Universities, foundations, and even the government were unable to escape the craze. Universities increased the study of Latin America, gave more scholarships to Latin students and sent more professors south to do research. The foundations plunged into cultural exchanges in every field imaginable. And the federal government soon had so many agencies concerned with Latin activities that Roosevelt found it necessary to appoint a Coordinator of Inter-American affairs. It was the start of the public career of Nelson A. Rockefeller, frequent aspirant to the Republican nomination for President and four-times Governor of New York.

It is always hard to detect the cause of those fads that successively convulse the United States like a fever, but one factor was certainly the approach of World War II in Europe. This cut down U.S.–European contacts and made Latin America so much more important to the United States as trading partner, source of raw materials, and as an area crucial to American security.

Increasingly the approaching war influenced U.S.–Latin American relations. By the end of 1938 when the clouds of war were gathering over Europe, the American nations met at Lima, Peru. In recent months Germany, Italy, and Japan—all of whom had large numbers of nationals in Latin America— had been conducting propaganda campaigns aimed at separating the Latin nations from the United States. With this background most of the Latin nations were, for a change, not concerned about their giant neighbor to the north. The United States took advantage of the general concern with the situation in Europe to push for what came to be called the Declaration of Lima. The twenty-one republics declared:

First. That they reaffirm their continental solidarity and their purpose to collaborate in the maintenance of the principles upon which the said solidarity is based.

Second. That faithful to the above-mentioned principles and to their absolute sovereignty, they reaffirm their decision to maintain them and to defend them against all foreign intervention or activity that may threaten them.

Third. And in case the peace, security or territorial integrity of any American Republic is thus threatened by acts of any nature that may impair them, they proclaim their common concern and their determination to make effective their solidarity, coordinating their respective sovereign wills by means of the procedure of consultation, established by conventions in force and by declarations of the Inter-American Conferences, using the measures which in each case the circumstances may make advisable. It is understood that the Governments of the American Republics will act independently in their individual capacity, recognizing fully their juridical equality as sovereign states.

Fourth. That in order to facilitate consultations established in this or any other American peace instrument, the Ministers for Foreign Affairs of the American Republics, when deemed desirable and at the initiative of any of them, will meet in their several capitals by rotation and without protocolary character. Each Government may, under special circumstances or for special reasons, designate a representative to substitute for its Minister for Foreign Affairs. . . .[7]

As soon as war broke out in Europe, nine nations called for an immediate conference of foreign ministers. The twenty-one nations met swiftly at Panama from September 23 to October 3, 1939. The American goal was clear: to line up the Latin nations in a neutrality favorable to Britain and France. The Latin nations were receptive, and the conference adopted a series of measures that enabled the individual countries, although theoretically neutral, to take actions that would benefit Britain and France and handicap Germany and Italy. These actions included trade, the sale of arms, the use of ships to transport goods to the belligerents, the reception of foreign warships, etc.

As triumphant German armies marched through Western Europe, U.S. concern increased further with the fear that Dutch or French colonies in or along the Caribbean might fall into German hands. On June 18, 1940, at the urging of Secretary Hull, Congress passed a joint resolution that "the United States would not recognize any transfer, and would not acquiesce in any attempt to transfer, any geographic region of this hemisphere from one non-American power to another non-American power. . . ." [8] The United States was reviving the no-transfer language of more than a century before, only this time it had infinitely more power to enforce it. Although German submarine bases in the Caribbean would have presented a serious danger, there was little likelihood that Germany would try to establish such bases, and even less likelihood that it could succeed.

Nonetheless, it was only prudent for the United States to make sure. At a second meeting of foreign ministers, in Havana, July 21–30, 1940, Hull finally succeeded in the full Pan-Americanization of the region's diplomacy. As the historian Bemis put it, "Declaration No. XV embodied the all-for-one-and-one-for-all principle . . . for which the United States had worked for so many years. . . ." It stipulated:

That any attempt on the part of a non-American State against the integrity or inviolability of the territory, the sovereignty or the political independence of an American State shall be considered as an act of aggression against the States which sign this declaration.

In case acts of aggression are committed or should there be reason to believe that an act of aggression is being prepared by a non-American nation against the integrity or inviolability of the territory, the sovereignty or the political independence of an American nation, the nations signatory to the present declaration will consult among themselves in order to agree upon the measures it may be advisable to take.

All the signatory nations, or two or more of them, according to circumstances, shall proceed to negotiate the necessary complementary agreements so as to organize cooperation for defense and the assistance that they shall lend each other in the event of aggressions such as referred to in the declaration.[9]

This declaration was the basis for the mutual defense agreements that the United States was to negotiate with various Latin nations just before and during American participation in the Second World War. However, it must be pointed out again that this one-for-all-and-all-for-one principle has long had two interpretations. The one prevalent in the United States is that this is an entirely reasonable arrangement for the mutual benefit of all the American states. The other view, held by critics of American foreign policy, is that such an arrangement makes the Latin nations the tail on the American kite.

Soon after Japan bombed Pearl Harbor on December 7, 1941, a number of Latin nations entered the war on the side of the United States and all of them, with the exception of Argentina and, to a lesser degree, Chile, cooperated enthusiastically with the United States. Both these nations flirted with the fascist regimes of Spain, Germany, and Italy; and Argentina openly helped the fascists until American and British pressure became too strong. American bases were established in Brazil, Mexico, Cuba, Panama, and Ecuador, and Latin America became a major source of supply of strategic materials such as rubber, minerals, and foodstuffs. Some humorous historians have characterized wartime U.S.–Latin American relations this way: Columbus discovered Latin America in 1492; the United States discovered it in 1942.

9

Latin America
and the Cold War

The Second World War, in many ways, benefited Latin America. It ended the depression that had affected the region so cruelly. It provided lucrative markets for its raw materials, and it forced the Latin nations to diversify their economies to some extent because the war sharply cut down the supply of industrial goods from abroad. On the other hand, the Latin economies remained largely dependent on the sale abroad of a few primary commodities. The wealth flowing into the countries as a result of wartime sales remained largely in the hands of the privileged few, and American investment in the region, already great, increased. Nonetheless, as the war came to an end there was reason to believe in Latin America that with the re-election of Good Neighbor Roosevelt in 1944 that relations between north and south would continue to improve.

But on April 12, 1945, less than a month before Germany surrendered, Franklin Delano Roosevelt died. No one can say whether he might have prevented the Cold War—that long, bitter, and costly struggle between the United States and the Soviet Union that was not quite war but certainly was far from peace. The Cold War was to have a profound influence on Latin America, but it is beyond the scope of this book to discuss in detail its origins.[1]

Briefly stated, there are three main schools of thought. The first, one that prevailed with little opposition in this country until the mid-1960s, was that the Soviet Union was almost entirely responsible. A second, and growing, school has argued in recent years that the United States was largely responsible. A third argues that given the history, tradition, and nature of the United States and the Soviet Union, and given the circumstances of a war-torn world, conflict was inevitable between the nations that had survived the terrible war as the world's two strongest powers. This is a debate among historians that will continue for generations. But however the Cold War started, the fact is indisputable that it dominated American policy toward Latin America.

The world was different in 1945. The gigantic upheavals of the Second World War had fatally weakened the empires of Britain and France. The peoples of their vast colonial lands in Africa and Asia were clamoring to be their own masters. There was no way to isolate this contagious virus of freedom. Inevitably it spread to Latin America as well. Paradoxically, the problem was more difficult there because the nations were already independent. There was no way that Britain or France or Holland, pushed by necessity and urged on by the United Nations, could give their subject peoples freedom with the stroke of a pen. In theory the people of Latin America were already free, but that, despite the nobility of the democratic language in their constitutions, was a cruel illusion. The

great masses were powerless, their fate in the hands of a privileged few who had demonstrated little desire to share the
wealth with the people whose labor made it possible. Only in
Mexico, more than thirty years before, had there been a genuine social revolution. The Indians, the blacks, those of mixed
parentage were still being exploited in most of Latin America.
They could not look to London and Paris, and the United Nations, for freedom. If they were to get it, it had to be obtained,
willingly or not, from their own privileged countrymen. This
transfer of power, successful or not, violent or not, would be
the history of Latin America in the decades after the end of
World War II. Thus, the old Good Neighbor Policy, even if it
were resumed, would not be enough, not nearly enough.

It was not until this postwar period, when good neighborliness required positive measures of economic and financial aid and a spirit
of understanding and sympathy with social and industrial revolutions and with the democratic aspirations that gathered force against
the military dictators, that the Good Neighbor policy, as distinct
from the policy of continental security, became difficult.[2]

Thus, two great historic forces came into opposition. The
United States was preoccupied with what it saw as the Communist menace at a time when the peoples of Latin America
were beginning to demand a better life. These two forces did
not have to be in opposition but, given the circumstances, it
was almost inevitable that they collide. This was tragic, not
only for the people of Latin America, but for the United States
as well, for its preoccupation with Communism caused it to
turn its back on its own principles.

For decades the United States, with genuine conviction, had
espoused the cause of democracy in Latin America. This, had

circumstances been different, could well have coincided with that region's great thrust for self-determination. But successive American presidents, from Truman to Nixon, have been convinced themselves that Communism in Latin America was a mortal threat to American security. Until recently this was seldom challenged in the United States, but in increasing numbers critics have begun to ask why developments within a sovereign nation should be any threat to the United States. These critics have asked why nations, even if they be in Latin America, should not have the right to have any kind of government they choose, even Communism. They wonder what right the United States has to judge the internal affairs of another nation, and they conclude that there is no basis in morality or in international law (particularly since the nonintervention agreements) for the United States to take action against an independent nation until such time that its policies constitute a clear and present danger to the United States. This, of course, parallels the thinking of the Latin American noninterventionists over the last century.

There is another school of thought. This would argue that Communism in Latin America may well be a threat to the United States, but that the best way to combat Communism is to combat the conditions—poverty, ignorance, disease, and most important, the feeling that one doesn't count—that make Communism possible. All the American administrations have said that they want democratic governments in Latin America, but the history of the past quarter-century proves that Washington has usually been quite content to deal with, entertain, and even decorate a clutch of repressive dictators—among them Rafael Trujillo of the Dominican Republic, Fulgencio Batista of Cuba, Pérez Jiménez of Venezuela, Anas-

tasio Somoza and his sons in Nicaragua, Getúlio Vargas of
Brazil, and Alfredo Stroessner of Paraguay. The reason is simple. These dictators were and are shrewd men. They immediately recognized Washington's preoccupation with Communism and perceived how they could exploit it to their own
advantage. They quickly swore loyalty to the anti-Communist
campaign, promised to ban Communism from their shores (an
easy promise since they were opposed to all change, Communist, democratic, or whatever) and instructed their diplomats
to vote with the United States on Cold War issues at the
United Nations and within the Organization of American
States.

From that it was inevitable that Washington would decide
that it was in its interest to provide the right-wing dictators'
armies with weapons and military advisers. This would provide defense against the Communists. However, it has never
been clear why the Latin nations needed big, well-equipped
armies. They had no external foes within Latin America and
the United States provided complete defense against any possible (but extremely unlikely) attack from outside the region—
except, of course, against an attack from the United States itself, as Guatemala and Cuba were to learn in the 1960s. But
since in the postwar years there *was* no real external danger, a
Latin American arms race developed out of a sense of national
prestige. Your army had to be as good as your neighbor's and
preferably a little better, even though neither of you had the
faintest notion of fighting one another.

There were two serious, and related, hazards to this unjus-
tified arms buildup. First, even with handsome American aid,
armies cost irreplaceable money desperately needed for economic development. Second, this strengthened the power of

the dictator and made it possible for him to be even less responsive to the legitimate grievances of his people. This obviously antagonized those groups within the various countries seeking change and caused the United States to be identified with the people of the past against the people of the future. Although this might have served Washington's short-term goal of anti-Communism, it could hardly have served the essential long-term goal of friendship with America's neighbors.

All this, of course, is a generalization. There are twenty Latin American states and some of them in the first decades after World War II had democratic governments for much or all of the time. Mexico, Costa Rica, Chile, Uruguay, and perhaps one or two others have had largely or entirely democratic rule. But most of the others much of the time have been ruled by dictators or oligarchies, almost invariably with military support.

Although it is possible to make generalizations about most Latin dictators, one unique ruler was Juan Perón of Argentina. From 1943 to 1955 his rule, shared by his wife, Eva, was almost absolute. But he, unlike most dictators, was not a representative of the oligarchy. Rather he rose to, and remained in, power by his demagogic manipulation of Argentina's large and influential labor unions. He and his wife, to their credit, did initiate reforms in wide areas of social welfare, and Perón did resume national control of large segments of the economy that had been under foreign control. But he overreached himself with grandiose economic development schemes that existed more on paper than in fact, and which angered the rural oligarchs. His foreign policy was anti-American and yet he was able to arrange enormous loans from the United States, which probably feared he would be even more anti-American if Washington did not come through. He also made Argentina a refuge for fascists fleeing Europe after the war.

By 1952 Perón's rule began to crumble. The wildly popular Eva, Evita to the crowds, died and the bankruptcy of Perón's economic policies became evident. He silenced the press by expropriation after trying to do so by bribes, withholding newsprint, and mob attacks. He resorted to increasing repression. Finally the Catholic Church, which had long supported him, turned against him. He responded with antichurch acts—legalizing divorce, proposing to end church participation in education, threatening complete separation of church and state and even taxing church property. *Peronista* mobs attacked the churches and when two high churchmen protested, they were exiled. The Vatican responded by excommunicating the dictator. Riots and counterriots broke out. On September 19, 1955, a military coup finally unseated Perón and he fled the country, first to Paraguay and then to Spain. Ecstatic mobs, many of whom had earlier rioted in support of Juan and Eva Perón, now toppled their statues and ripped down their posters. But after a period of democracy under Arturo Frondizi, chosen President of Argentina in 1958 by the first free election since 1916, the military resumed control of the country.

The first major event in U.S.–Latin American relations after the war was the Treaty of Rio in 1947. It was considered so important to the security of the United States that President Harry Truman flew to Brazil to address the closing session. Although the Latin nations at war's end were more concerned with economic development than with a military alliance and hoped for substantial American aid, the United States declined any substantial discussion of economic matters. Concerned with what it saw as a threat from Communist Russia, the United States wanted a military pact to secure its flank in the Western Hemisphere. The Rio Treaty provided that the American states would try to settle among themselves any hemispheric controversy before it went to the United Nations. This has always been a major goal of U.S. foreign policy, even in the early days of the United Nations when the United States had almost unchallenged dominance within the world body. Washington preferred to keep hemispheric disputes within the family free from what might be unwelcome interference by outsiders. Some have argued that this weakened the United Nations, which was intended to be the primary peacekeeping organization.

The Rio Treaty covered not only armed attack but a wide range of contingencies: ". . . any aggression which is not an armed attack or by an extra-continental or intra-continental conflict or by any other fact or situation that might endanger the peace of America. . . ." This meant that the United States, or any other nation, could invoke the treaty in almost any controversy.

If such a controversy should arise, the treaty's Organ of Consultation would meet immediately to consider what measures to take. These measures could include economic sanctions or even armed force. A two-thirds vote would be necessary and, if obtained, would "be binding upon all the signatory States . . . with the sole exception that no State shall be required to use armed force without its consent. . . ." Thus, the American states gave to themselves the same powers as existed in the Charter of the United Nations, allowing them to avoid that organization if they chose.

Pan-Americanization reached its high point the following year, 1948, when the Organization of American States was

founded at Bogotá, Colombia. Again the Latin states were
seeking substantial U.S. economic aid, particularly since the
United States had already begun, with the Marshall Plan, a
massive aid program for war-torn Europe. Secretary of State
George C. Marshall himself headed the American delegation.
But he was interested primarily in establishing an inter-American defense against Communism. He succeeded and the
Latin statesmen who sought economic aid did not. Whereas
Washington's preoccupation with Communism had been tacit
at Rio, it was made explicit at Bogotá. In a resolution on the
"Preservation and Defense of Democracy in America," it was
proclaimed that "because of its anti-democratic nature and in-
terventionistic tendency, the political action of international
Communism or of any totalitarianism is incompatible with the
concept of American freedom." The resolution also called for
"urgent measures . . . to prevent the agents of international
Communism or of any other totalitarianism from trying to un-
dermine the free and authentic will of the peoples of this continent." This, of course, made it easy for the many dictators in
Latin America to label any opposition movement as Communist and ask the United States for aid. And it was ironic that a
document promoting freedom and self-determination was approved by a whole clutch of dictators who ruthlessly attempted
to smash every endeavor by their people to win freedom and
self-determination. Unfortunately, Washington often demonstrated a readiness to see any opposition as Communist-led
even when it wasn't. And beyond that lies the basic question:
does a people have the right to choose any kind of government
it wants, even Communist?

The United States had thus established at Bogotá the firm
base of its anti-Communist foreign policy for Latin America.

In succeeding years it would augment that base by the establishment of military missions in almost every Latin nation and the large-scale provision of military assistance to most of them.

But even so stalwart an anti-Communist as Sumner Welles questioned the results of the Bogotá Conference.

What guarantee do we have that permits us to suppose that a form of democracy that has evolved gradually to meet the needs of the English-speaking nations should for that reason answer in identical fashion the needs of peoples with absolutely different origins, traditions and cultures? If we seek now to restrict the right of the peoples of Latin America to support or overthrow their own governments, we will be destroying the regional system of the New World.[3]

Yet as demonstrated by Welles himself in Cuba in 1933–1934 and by Wilson, Taft, and Teddy Roosevelt earlier, the United States had long believed that it had the right to approve or disapprove of revolutions in Latin America.

Although there are instances beyond number of American presidents welcoming Latin dictators, of American ambassadors becoming their intimate friends, of American military men helping their Latin colleagues to put down opposition, one instance will suffice here to demonstrate how such behavior served to discredit the United States in the eyes of Latin American reformers and harm this country in the long run. In Venezuela, in 1950, Colonel Marcos Pérez Jiménez seized power. He held it for eight years. Although he did make some economic improvements, he brutally crushed all opposition. He welcomed foreign investments, offering lenient tax policies. American investment grew, enjoying not only the dictator's tax benefits but the ruthlessly imposed stability. He became popular in Washington and President Dwight D. Eisenhower conferred upon him the order of the Legion of Merit. Finally, in January of 1958, reformers drove him, now rich beyond belief, into exile. Since this kind of warm relationship between Latin dictators and successive administrations in Washington has often existed throughout the century, it is inevitable that many Latin reformers have seen the United States as more enemy than friend.

In 1951, after North Korea had invaded South Korea, the United States tried to get the Latin nations to send troops to fight in Korea. Most offered token contingents, but only Colombia met the UN request to send a force of at least a thousand men. Many Latin leaders opposed Communism within the continent, either out of genuine conviction and/or because it was easy to label domestic opposition as Communist. But many of these same leaders saw the Cold War between the United States and the Soviet Union—of which the Korean War was a deadly episode—as no concern of theirs except to the degree that it affected Latin America directly. And this was largely as a means of exploiting Washington's fears to gain military, economic, and political assistance as good anti-Communist allies.

In the early 1950s, the United States departed for once from its customary practice and actively helped a group of revolutionists. The country was Bolivia and the revolutionary leader was Victor Paz Estenssoro, a lawyer and professor of economics. He and his colleagues proposed wide-ranging reforms, including nationalizing the tin mines (the chief source of foreign exchange), giving the vote to illiterate Indians (a majority of the nation), and distributing land widely to peasant farms. Paz's party, aided by more extreme left-wing groups, won the 1951 elections, but the conservative "tin barons" and large landowners joined with the military in preventing Paz from taking office as President. It seemed that once again the oligarchy had blocked reform.

This time, however, it was different. The mineworkers had arms and, led by a star soccer player, Juan Lechín, joined Paz's party in attacking the ruling military junta. After fierce fighting, the junta surrendered and Paz returned from exile to take office. He knew that the sweeping reforms he had proposed would be difficult because Bolivia lacked sufficient money and trained technicians to carry them out successfully. But he also knew that if he did not push the reforms through at once, they might never be achieved. So he went ahead. It was fully as difficult as he had feared, and the revolution might have collapsed in the early years had not the United States stepped in with substantial economic assistance.

When Paz returned to Bolivia in 1952, the United States recognized that he was a capable leader and it feared that if his reforms failed, chaos and confusion might lead to the dreaded Communism. So the United States gave considerable help, even though some of the leading members of the government were Marxists openly critical of the United States, and even though the tin mines were nationalized, a course that Washington seldom welcomes. Eventually, as is usually the case in Latin America, the lack of the tradition and structure of democratic government proved fatal to the Paz regime. With dissension within his party, with the tin miners demanding more pay, Paz became more autocratic. Then, like many other Latin American reformers before him (and after), he had the Constitution amended so he could be nominated for re-election to another term. This outraged many of his own supporters who feared that Paz wanted to become another lifetime dictator.

Time and time again this has happened in Latin America.

A reformer with a genuine desire to establish democracy has found it impossible to do so within his term of office. The idealistic and democratic constitutions written by reformers almost invariably limit the time in office of a president because they fear a long time will inevitably mean dictatorship. Thus, when a reformer reaches the end of his term and finds no structure to carry on his reforms, he has two choices: to step out of office and let the old chaotic struggle for power return, or attempt to change his own Constitution to remain in power. If he takes this latter course, he often fails because he alienates his own supporters; if he succeeds, he has become the kind of dictator, even if a benevolent one, he fought to throw out of office. The struggle to effect change in Latin America, therefore, is a slow and difficult one, with often as many setbacks as advances.

In the case of Paz, he was overthrown in November 1964 by his Vice-President, General René Barrientos, a U.S.-trained air force officer. Here, however, is a departure from the old script. Barrientos was not an ally of the old oligarchy; he was young and trained in the United States. His ideas were more modern than the old rule-and-profit idea of the traditional Latin military, and he was determined to carry on the revolution, as have been his military successors. Barrientos and his successors are representative of a new breed of Latin military men who, professional and receptive to the ideas of the time, often see themselves as more fit to govern in the national interest than the oligarchies. They are often nationalistic and suspicious of the United States and willing to undertake political, social, and economic reforms that horrify the traditional, right-wing military. Although such governments as Barrientos' existed in mid-1971 in Bolivia and Peru, there were even more of the old-style military governments, so it is too soon to predict that these new-style nationalist-reformist military movements will prevail. That such caution is justified was demonstrated in August 1971 when more conservative military forces overthrew the left-wing government of General Juan José Torres Gonzales.

Shortly after the United States decided in 1953 to help the reformer Paz, it had a similar opportunity in Guatemala. Here, however, it reverted to more characteristic behavior. For decades Guatemala had been governed by a series of harsh dictators with occasional periods of less repressive rule. From 1931 to 1944, the dictator was General Jorge Ubico. Though as President he established financial stability and political order, and increased health and school facilities, his methods were arbitrary. He sternly suppressed opposition, warning potential enemies, "I execute first and give trial afterward." [4]

After Ubico was overthrown by a military junta, Juan Arevalo was easily elected President. He abolished forced labor on the banana plantations owned mainly by the United Fruit Company of Boston, raised the minimum wage to twenty-six cents a day, permitted unions, and tried to liberate the country's economy from its near-total dependence on United Fruit and other foreign companies. Despite the fact that the country was stagnating and desperately needed changes, the old ruling class and the foreign investers opposed Arevalo's programs. Following the customary practice, Arevalo was accused of being a Communist, and in his first four years more than two dozen attempts were made to oust him. By 1950 the attempts to overthrow him were growing more serious. He asked American Ambassador Richard C. Patterson to leave because he openly sympathized with the conspirators and because he had publicly accused Arevalo of "persecution of American business."

In reprisal, U.S. business firms cut down their operations in Guatemala. Banana exports, for instance, plunged 80 per cent between 1948 and 1952. The United States cut off military assistance and the World Bank, dominated by the United States, withheld loans. Worse was to come, when Arevalo was succeeded by Jacobo Arbenz Guzmán. Arbenz, a member of the junta that had overthrown the dictator Ubico, won by almost twice as many votes as all the other candidates together. He, too, wanted drastic reforms and he, too, was willing to use local Communists in the government. Arbenz' pet project was land reform, necessary in a country where about 2 per cent of the population owned 70 per cent of the land. In March 1953, Arbenz expropriated 234,000 acres of uncultivated land from United Fruit. The Boston firm demanded almost $16 million in compensation but Arbenz offered only $600,000—the value the company had declared for tax purposes. The U.S. State Department, now headed by John Foster Dulles, intervened and supported United Fruit's claim.

Washington then began a campaign against Arbenz, asserting that Communism was taking over in Latin America with Guatemala as the beachhead. The State Department issued a white paper accusing Arbenz of implicitly accepting Communists as "an authentic domestic political party and not as part of the world-wide Soviet Communist conspiracy." [5] It is true that Arbenz used Communists in his government. He, like many other persons all over the world, did not accept the American contention that local Communists put Moscow over loyalty to their own nation. There were perhaps three thousand Communists in Guatemala out of a population of three million. Although they did hold a number of important government posts, they were not represented in the Cabinet and had only four seats in the Congress. It appears true, however, that Arbenz had a number of Communists as close friends and that he relied on them as "the leading source of ideas and political energy in the country." It also appears that a few top Guatemalan Communists took continuing direction from Moscow, but while they sought to deal with genuine local concerns, they had neither a revolutionary program nor a broad local constituency.

This is how Richard J. Barnet sums up Communist influence in his fine *Intervention and Revolution*:

. . . Guatemala was far from adopting a Communist economy or social system. She was receiving no aid from the Soviet Union or indeed had any relationship with the Communist bloc. Arbenz was actually using the Communists to help administer a continuation of the moderate reformist program of Arevalo, who was a rather strong anti-Communist. Arbenz's program of nationalization was neither more rapid nor more onerous than those of other non-Communist countries of Latin America and Asia. The cry of Communist had been the traditional pretext for opposing reformers in Guatemala. Now that both the pace of reform and the participation of Communists had been stepped up, anti-Communism reached hysterical proportions.[6]

Following in its long tradition, Washington decided that Communists could not be permitted to participate in the political life of Guatemala. The Central Intelligence Agency was assigned to overthrow the Arbenz government, but first the political stage had to be set in Latin America. In March 1954, John Foster Dulles went to Caracas, Venezuela, where the tenth Pan-American Conference was taking place. He rammed through a tough anti-Communist resolution that read, in part:

. . . That the domination or control of the political institutions of any American state by the international Communist movement, extending to this hemisphere the political system of an extra-continental power, would constitute a threat to the sovereignty and political independence of the American States, endangering the peace of America, and would call for a meeting of consultation to consider the adoption of appropriate action in accordance with existing treaties.[7]

It was perfectly clear whom this resolution was aimed at: Guatemala. Gautemala, of course, voted against the resolution and Argentina and Mexico abstained. The Mexican delegation declared:

Mexico will not support the proposal of the United States with its affirmative vote because the form in which it is worded could give rise to interventions in any of our countries, such as no American state should suffer. . . . We are afraid that future interpretation of this document might contain elements that could provoke intervention against a government which is accused of being Communist merely because it tries, fully within its rights, to win its economic independence and to combat capitalist interests within its own territory. This is not purely hypothetical: we have seen it happen in the past. Mexico has suffered interventions in its territory and these have been extra-continental and by countries of this hemisphere. We know what we are talking about; we know that if we want American unity it is impossible to leave the door open so that intervention may be resorted to again at any given moment.[8]

As soon as Dulles got the resolution he wanted, he left Caracas, even though the conference still had two weeks to go and the most important matters, from the Latin point of view, were still to come.

A few months later, in mid-June 1954, in a sort of dress rehearsal for the 1961 Bay of Pigs operation in Cuba, U.S. pilots in U.S. planes bombed Guatemala City. Colonel Castillo Armas led a tiny band of exiles across the border, mercenaries recruited, trained, and paid by the Central Intelligence Agency. This tiny force could easily have been defeated, but the Guatemalan army refused to support Arbenz or to allow him to distribute arms to the people. Not only was the army itself worried about the Communists in the Arbenz government, but the American air raid gave them notice that the United States was not going to permit Arbenz to stay in power. The military wanted to stay on Washington's good side.

Arbenz capitulated on June 27, and a couple of days later Dulles reported in a television address that the situation was "being cured by the Guatemalans themselves." And at the United Nations, Ambassador Henry Cabot Lodge said the United States had had nothing to do with the affair.

Armas, of course, became President and the United States, which in previous years had given Guatemala only a few hundred thousand dollars exclusive of road subsidies, poured $90 million into Guatemala in the next two years to bolster its chosen President. Armas promptly returned the expropriated lands to United Fruit, which had actively helped in the operation to overthrow Arbenz, and made changes in the tax laws that quickly saved United Fruit about $11 million. He also threw more than five thousand political opponents into jail, abolished the secret ballot, and disenfranchised the "illiterate masses," about 70 per cent. He then went on to win, in a one-candidate election, what President Eisenhower in his memoirs called a "thundering majority."

Only later did it become clear that the Eisenhower administration had engineered Arbenz's ouster, a clear violation of the nonintervention clauses of a number of binding international agreements. But apart from that, what can be said of the American intervention? As with earlier interventions, the only way to make a judgment is to examine its long-term effects. Armas was assassinated in 1957 and Guatemala has been in turmoil since. A brutal and bloody struggle of revolution and counterrevolution has gone on to this day, with both sides engaged in appalling violence and the dead numbering in the many hundreds.

The United States has assisted successive governments in trying to put down the rebels. This, no doubt, was the rationalization used by terrorists to justify the murder in 1968 of the American ambassador and two U.S. aides. Terrorists have also kidnapped a number of foreign diplomats, among them the West German ambassador, who was killed in 1970 when the government would not make concessions to the rebels. The government, at this writing, was headed by Carlos Arana Osorio, who had pledged to put down the rebellion by relentless repression. No one can predict what will happen in Guatemala, but it is safe to say that violence of the most extreme nature will continue. One can wonder what the Arbenz government might have done that would have been worse than what has followed his ouster by the United States.

After the Guatemalan adventure, the Eisenhower administration largely turned its back on Latin America until a series of dramatic and frightening events in the spring of 1958. Eisenhower had sent Vice-President Richard M. Nixon on a goodwill tour of eight Latin American nations. His reception was a drastic departure from normal Latin hospitality. In some cities he was greeted by riots and epithets, and in Caracas, Venezuela, on May 13 he was spat upon and almost mobbed. He stood his ground bravely, but it was only with this explosion that Washington realized how much its Latin American relations had deteriorated. For too long the United States had allied itself with dictators and for too long it had refused to consider the massive aid needed by its southern neighbors. No doubt Communists and leftists helped whip up anti-American feelings into demonstrations and riots, but the feeling was there to be whipped up.

A few months later President Eisenhower sent his brother Milton, a distinguished educator, to Latin America to solicit the views of political leaders. John Foster Dulles was sent to Brazil to discuss with President Juscelino Kubitschek his proposed Operation Pan America which was a forerunner of John Kennedy's Alliance for Progress. The United States participated in a number of inter-American meetings and withdrew its objection to a new lending agency, the Inter-American Development Bank, which was chartered in 1959 and began operation the following year. In September 1960 at Bogotá, the twenty-one American nations agreed on a concerted attack on the social and economic causes of underdevelopment. The Inter-American Development Bank was to provide funds to those countries willing to make genuine economic and social reforms. The Eisenhower administration pledged an initial $500 million to underwrite the program. At last after years of disagreement, often bitter, between the United States and its southern neighbors, agreement had been reached on the principle that the United States must offer massive aid. But, as we shall soon see, despite the promise of the Alliance for Progress that was to be born a few months later, little was to come of this proposal for a great continental effort to improve the lives of millions of Latin Americans.

10

The United States
vs. Cuba

Obviously a mighty nation has a profound influence on a weaker nation, but at two watershed moments in U.S. history, it has been a small and dependent country, Cuba, that was the focal point of decisive events. The Spanish–American War in Cuba in 1898 set the United States on the course of empire, and the 1962 Cuban missile crisis was to take the United States and Russia to the brink of the nuclear war that man has dreaded since the first atomic bomb exploded over Hiroshima.

Even though the United States could no longer directly intervene in Cuban affairs after 1934, American investments continued to grow to such an extent, particularly in sugar, Cuba's most important export, that Cuba was generally regarded as an economic colony. Although the American investments and American–Cuban trade brought a kind of prosperity to the island, it was a lopsided prosperity. Statistically, Cuba had the highest standard of living in Latin America. There was, for instance, the highest per capita proportion of automobiles in the region. But this prosperity was enjoyed only by a small percentage of the Cubans, those who were closely allied with the Americans. Most Cubans, those whose labor in the cane fields and the sugar mills produced the nation's wealth, lived in terrible poverty, as they had for centuries.

During most of these years Batista was the island's master in fact if not name, serving as the power behind the throne when he did not occupy the presidency himself. The American ambassador was often regarded as the second most powerful man in Havana, and U.S. investors had enormous influence. While they held power, Batista and his henchmen profited hugely. By corruption and outright theft they amassed great fortunes, did little to help the *campesinos,* and stamped out any flickerings of democracy or social and economic change that appeared. They allowed Havana to become one of the great vice capitals of the world, a refuge for American mobsters and a lure for American tourists seeking pleasures illegal in the United States.

Then in 1952, after a period of reduced influence, Batista returned to power, again with an army coup. With the passing years his regime grew increasingly repressive and brutal. Fidel Castro, a young middle-class lawyer, joined the opposition and as early as 1953 led an unsuccessful raid against a Batista headquarters. He was captured and exiled to Mexico but in 1956 returned to the forests of the Sierra Maestra in Cuba. From this mountain retreat he began a rebellion that grew slowly and never saw great numbers of men under arms. But Castro and his closest colleagues were able guerrilla leaders, and the rebellion weakened the Batista regime, which, despite an army vastly superior in numbers and equipment, never had sufficient resolve nor, certainly, sufficient popular support to undertake an effective campaign against Castro.

Batista followed the time-honored course of dictators. Rather than attempt to improve the conditions that were the basic cause of the rebellion, he resorted to violent repression. In time this embarrassed Washington, which had always supported Batista because of his fervent professions of anti-Communism, something of a paradox, for he had often worked with Cuban Communists when he needed their political support. By March of 1958 the Eisenhower administration cut off the supply of arms to Batista. This was a terrible blow, not so much because of the arms—he already had more than enough—but because it signaled the end of support from Washington, until then essential to any Cuban ruler.

The cutoff of American arms shipments foreshadowed the end of the Batista regime. Castro and his top lieutenants, his brother Raul and Ernesto "Che" Guevara, the Argentinian physician turned revolutionary, stepped up their raids. They struck quickly from the mountains, then melted away before Batista's troops could react. Although greatly outnumbered and outgunned, Castro and his men were courageous and bold and, most important, they had the support of the people. Batista increased the violence of his response. Rather than try to meet the aspirations of the people for a better life, he resorted to wholesale executions and murders. This only turned the people more against him and added recruits to Castro's small but growing forces.

Batista's regime began to collapse, as much a victim of its own corruption and lack of moral purpose as of Castro's armed rebellion. That is the way with most rebellions. They succeed only when a repressive government has lost the capacity to use effectively its greatly superior manpower and fire-power. In less than three years Castro's tiny band in the Sierra Maestra had toppled a large army and air force equipped with modern American weapons. As 1958 came to an end, Batista and his top aides fled to the Dominican Republic and from there to Portugal, already having made provisions for themselves to live in luxury for the rest of their lives. By January 1, 1959, Cuba belonged to Castro and his revolutionaries.

The following months and years were both chaotic and controversial. It is a period about which it is difficult to write objectively, for in the United States Castro was either a hero or a villain. Perhaps given the circumstances, the personalities, and the history of Cuban–American relations, a break was inevitable. One thing is certain. Whatever Castro may have had in mind when he first took to the hills, by the time he had achieved power he had decided on a real social and economic revolution, a sweeping revolution of a scope unknown in Latin America since the Mexican Revolution a half century before. This was not to be a revolution in name only, merely a reshuffling of the political figures at the top, with the new leaders eager to establish cordial relations with the Colossus of the North. Castro wanted profound changes, and any such changes, for better or worse, would mean breaking the economic grip of the American corporations. Yet it must be recognized that Cuba at this time had perhaps the highest per capita income of any Latin nation, more cars, more of almost all the economic indicators of prosperity. However, as Castro saw it, this relative wealth was entirely dependent upon the United States and was enjoyed by only a small proportion of the population.

Thus began a two-year period of move and countermove.

Castro would expropriate some American property under terms unsatisfactory to its owners, and Washington would take some economic reprisal. Cuba would move toward trade with Russia and Eastern Europe, and Washington would take an action that would handicap the Cuban economy. Supporters of each side would blame the other. Critics of Castro would argue that if he hadn't been a Communist all along, he was rapidly moving in that direction. Non-Communist supporters would argue that he was being forced into the arms of the Communists by the actions of the Eisenhower administration. It was a complex and controversial period with one's conclusions often depending upon one's point of view.

Whichever side was responsible (or perhaps both), a deep and bitter hostility was developing between Havana and Washington. The most severe blow came on July 6, 1960, when Eisenhower signed a bill cutting the Cuban sugar quota. Since the Cuban economy was almost entirely dependent on its sale of sugar to the United States, this was a declaration of economic warfare. As Eisenhower said, "This action amounts to economic sanctions against Castro. Now we must look ahead to other moves—economic, diplomatic, strategic." [1]

All during this period, middle-class Cuban supporters of Castro's revolution were becoming disillusioned. They had wanted Batista out but they had not bargained on a revolution as wide-ranging and as deep, one that amounted to a fundamental redistribution of the land's wealth. Although they were democrats, they were capitalists not socialists, and a form of socialism was what Castro had begun. Many of the middle-class Cubans fled to the United States, where they would participate, to a greater or less degree, in attempts to overthrow Castro.

This difficult period was also the period of a presidential campaign. Richard M. Nixon was the Republican candidate to succeed General Eisenhower, and John F. Kennedy was the Democratic candidate. Kennedy in a hard-hitting campaign pledged to "get the country moving again." He was particularly hard on the Eisenhower administration's foreign policy (although he seldom criticized directly the popular "Ike"), accusing it of not being tough enough on Communism, particularly of being too easy on Castro. This was a curious complaint, since the Eisenhower administration had undertaken a series of tough measures that cut at the very foundation of the Cuban economy. And Eisenhower broke diplomatic relations with Cuba just a few days before Kennedy took office.

Soon after he was elected, Kennedy was informed of the plan made months before for an invasion of Cuba by exiles recruited, paid, equipped, and trained by the U.S. Central Intelligence Agency. He gave the word to go ahead with the planning and training, saying he'd make a final decision after he took office. Such an invasion, aimed at Castro's overthrow, was, of course, prohibited by a series of binding nonintervention agreements to which the United States was a party.

Toward the end of 1960, Cuba, at the United Nations and elsewhere, accused the United States of planning such an invasion. The State Department, under Eisenhower and in the first weeks of the Kennedy administration, scoffed at such accusations as absurd. The American press, most notably the *New York Times,* also learned of the invasion, but at Kennedy's request suppressed the story.

The Bay of Pigs invasion merits fuller treatment than is possible here.[2] In brief, by early April 1961, Kennedy had decided to go ahead, and on April 17 about 1,500 brave exiles hit

the beach at the now-famous Bay of Pigs. They were preceded
by a bombardment from American planes flown by American
pilots. American frogmen were the first on the beach and then
came the Cubans, landed by American boats from American
ships. The invasion was a complete fiasco. The men, many of
them overage and without military experience, were poorly
trained. Castro's army and air force reacted far better than
American intelligence reports had expected and, most important, there was absolutely no sign of the anti-Castro uprising
that the C.I.A. had predicted. Many of the exiles were killed.
The rest, a large number of them wounded, were captured and
languished in Cuban prisons until ransomed by private American funds.

A furious storm of protest the world over greeted the news of
the failed invasion. As anti-Castroism was then popular in the
United States, much of the criticism from within the country
came because the operation had failed. Kennedy was criticized for believing 1,500 men, however brave, could overthrow
a well-trained, well-motivated, and forewarned military force
infinitely superior in numbers. But the most telling criticism
was more basic. Whether or not such an operation could succeed was not the point; it was fundamentally wrong for the
new President to intervene with armed force in the internal
affairs of an independent nation. The United States, these critics of Kennedy contended, did not have the right to dictate (or
try to) the form of government in a sovereign state.

Kennedy took the full blame for the operation's failure but
never conceded that he was wrong to violate the principle, and
the law, of nonintervention. Indeed, on April 20, 1961, Kennedy made a tough speech before the American Society of
Newspaper Editors. He seemed to depart from the facts by
saying:

. . . we made it repeatedly clear that the armed forces of this country would not intervene in any way.

Any unilateral American intervention, in the absence of an external attack upon ourselves or an ally, would have been contrary to our traditions and to our international obligations. . . .

But let the record show that our restraint is not inexhaustible. Should it ever appear that the inter-American doctrine of noninterference merely conceals or excuses a policy of nonaction—if the nations of this Hemisphere should fail to meet their commitments against outside Communist penetration—then I want it clearly understood that this Government will not hesitate in meeting its primary obligations which are to the security of our Nation! [3]

This would seem to be a sweeping extension of the Monroe Doctrine. The United States unilaterally now forbade not only intervention in the Western Hemisphere by a noncontinental power but the importation of a political philosophy.

Although John Kennedy was defeated in this attempt to overthrow the Castro government by force, he did not give up his anti-Castro campaign, even though it was solidifying the Castro government in Cuba and increasing its prestige throughout Latin America. Kennedy moved on the diplomatic, economic, and military fronts. Even before the Bay of Pigs, Kennedy had reduced the Cuban sugar quota to zero. Afterward, on September 7, Congress, with the President's approval, prohibited assistance to any country that aided Cuba, unless the President determined that such assistance was in the U.S. national interest.

There was little Cuba could do to respond to the American moves, but Castro hardly attempted to mollify Kennedy. On December 2, 1961, he declared: "I believe absolutely in Marxism. . . . I am a Marxist–Leninist and will be a Marxist–Leninist until the last day of my life." This reopened the old debate: had Castro been a secret Communist from the beginning (most evidence indicates he was not), did he willingly become a Communist because of the circumstances facing him after he took power, or was he pushed into Communism by the American crusade against him? Whatever conclusion one reaches, there is plenty of evidence that he was a Cuban first and a Communist second, that, unlike the Communist leaders in Eastern Europe, he was independent to a degree that must have often angered the Kremlin. However, Cuba did usually vote with the Soviet bloc at the United Nations.

Kennedy's campaign against Castro quickened early in 1962. A high-powered American delegation attended a conference of the Organization of American States at Punta del Este in Uruguay. Under strong American pressure the other states of the O.A.S. excluded Cuba from the organization. It was less than a total victory for Kennedy, however. The United States barely got the two-thirds majority to exclude Cuba (and there was considerable doubt that such an action was possible under O.A.S. rules), and the four largest and most important states— Argentina, Brazil, Chile, and Mexico—did not support the Americans. Fully half the votes came from nations ruled by right-wing dictators, and Haiti gave its essential vote only after the United States submitted to blackmail and promised to resume economic aid it had ended.[4] However, all the American states, other than Cuba, voted for a resolution asserting that Cuba's relationship with Russia was "incompatible" with the inter-American system. This declared that Cuba did not have the right to choose its friends as it saw fit, clearly an attempted infringement of that island nation's sovereignty.

Soon thereafter Kennedy declared an embargo on all trade

with Cuba except for medical necessities. Then the United States asked its fellow members in the North Atlantic Treaty Organization to take the O.A.S. decisions into account in determining their policies toward Cuba. Then the United States banned the importation of goods made in whole or in part from Cuban products.

This was the aspect of Kennedy's Latin American policy directed specifically at Castro. There was another, designed to prevent the conditions that might cause other Castros to arise in Latin America. The heart of this program was the Alliance for Progress, launched with such hope only a few weeks after Kennedy took office. This was to be a mighty, cooperative effort in which the United States would provide the money and the technical assistance, and the Latin nations themselves would make the political, economic, and social reforms necessary to any real progress. Some limited progress was made here and there, in school-building and health programs and the like. But the dreamed-of continental effort never came to much, and after Kennedy's death in November of 1963, it was allowed to expire quietly.

Part of the reason for the limited success was that Kennedy's characteristically American optimism had overestimated the degree to which vast assistance, even if maintained (which it was not), could influence problems as immense as those of Latin America. Population was growing so fast (the fastest in the world) that the area had to run at full speed to avoid going backwards. Further, the Alliance was plagued with bureaucratic problems from the beginning, both in Washington and the Latin capitals. The Latin nations just did not have the trained personnel to do so much so fast.

Just as important, perhaps more so, was a paradox built

right into the Alliance. Clearly the primary motivation for the program in Washington was to prevent the emergence of other Castros. (This is not to say, however, that there was not a genuine idealistic concern with raising the standard of living of the Latin peoples.) For Washington to be successful in taking a hard anti-Castro line in the O.A.S., it needed the votes of the right-wing dictators. Yet it was these very dictators who were most violently opposed to the kind of changes in their own society that were essential to any real and lasting progress. Kennedy genuinely wanted progressive liberals to rule in Latin America, yet his determination to contain Castro's revolution was so strong that he would not risk losing the dictators' support of capitalism by not supporting them. The Alliance for Progress was never able to overcome this self-contradiction, and the situation became worse when, in the years immediately after the birth of the Alliance, a half-dozen Latin states were recaptured by old-style military juntas.

There was also a military aspect to Kennedy's determination to prevent new Castros from arising. He decided to increase military aid to Latin America. This took the form not only of money and modern military equipment but, most significantly, the training of Latin officers and noncommissioned officers in antiguerrilla warfare at bases in Panama and the United States. Guerrilla-warfare specialists were also sent to advise Latin armies. This, of course, increased the ability of the governments in power, often unpopular dictators, to stay in power. And the program was continued by Presidents Johnson and Nixon. While in the short run it has had some success in keeping pro-American governments in power, it has often made bitter enemies of those who are struggling for change in such countries as Guatemala, Brazil, the Dominican Republic, and Bolivia. The Americans killed, kidnapped, or injured by rebels have often been those engaged in antiguerrilla warfare or training. In Guatemala, for instance, the American ambassador, John Mein, was killed in 1968, as were two U.S. military men. They were accused by left-wing rebels of aiding the right-wing government in its repression of revolutionary forces.

Many critics of American foreign policy, at home and abroad, have argued that the United States often takes the side in Latin America of the few against the many. There has been much written in recent years about rising anti-Americanism in Latin America. The main factor in this may well be the belief that Washington is usually on the side of the masters and not the masses. In the long run the United States may come to regret that it has become identified with the powerful "ins" who represent the past and not the aspiring "outs" who represent the future.

The conflict between Kennedy (with his enormous resources) and Castro (who had almost no material resources but who flew the banner of revolution in a continent ripe for it) led to one of the most dangerous moments in the history of the world, the Cuban missile crisis of 1962.

Although there is absolutely no reason to believe that Kennedy was even contemplating another armed attack on Cuba, there is every reason to believe that Castro was genuinely afraid that such an attempt might occur. It must be remembered that by early 1962 Kennedy had initiated a whole series of tough economic and diplomatic measures against Cuba. Sometime in mid-1962, Castro either asked for or Premier Nikita Khrushchev offered Russian missiles to be based on Cuba.

This was a serious mistake. However genuine was their

alarm that Cuba might be invaded, other measures could have been used as a serious deterrent against any possible American attack. The two nations could have signed a defense alliance, or the Russians could have sent symbolic contingents of Soviet troops, either or both coupled with a stern announcement from the Kremlin that an attack on Cuba would be regarded as an attack on the Soviet Union. For Khrushchev should have known that no American president, particularly one of Kennedy's assertive temperament, could have permitted Soviet missiles so close to U.S. soil in an area that for a century and a half had been regarded as an American preserve. This even though American missiles had long been in Turkey, right next door to Russia. However unfair this may have seemed to the Russians or (as it did) to many others, even friends of the United States, such was the mood of the American people that any president who permitted such an act would have suffered serious, probably fatal, political damage.

Nonetheless, while asserting frequently that only defensive weapons were being sent to Cuba, Khrushchev sent missiles of considerable range and began to construct launching sites. By the end of summer reports began to circulate in the United States that there might be missile sites. On September 4, 1962, Kennedy declared that there was no evidence of Russian missiles or any other "significant offensive capability." But he warned, "Were it to be otherwise, the gravest issues would arise." Three days later the President requested authority from Congress to call up 150,000 reserves if needed. On September 11, Russia warned that any attack by the United States on Cuba or on Soviet ships bound to Cuba would mean war, implying that it meant nuclear war.

The two great nations were heading to the brink. The

United States now was sending U-2s (extremely high altitude photo reconnaissance planes) over Cuba, but bad weather obscured much of the island and it was not until October 14 that photos were obtained of missile sites. It took a day to study and interpret them, and on October 16, Kennedy was informed that the reports were true, there were Soviet missile sites on Cuba. His first reaction was that prompt military action was required.[5] He immediately summoned into being a special group of high-level advisers, later called the Executive Committee, or ExCom. They quickly decided, with Kennedy's approval, not to seek a diplomatic solution to the crisis. Khrushchev would have to be forced to remove the missiles.

There was no real fear that the missiles would be used against the United States, for Khrushchev surely recognized that to use the missiles would mean a nuclear retaliation against the Soviet Union. Nor would the missiles have had much influence on the military balance of power. Russia already had a formidable array of nuclear missiles in Russia aimed at the United States, and in any case the United States was still far superior in nuclear strength. The main concern was that the installation of missiles would give Khrushchev, and Castro, a great political and psychological boost. Kennedy would not permit that. The question was not whether the missiles should go, but how to make them go.

Two crucial points must be discussed here. However unwise it was of Khrushchev to send Russian rockets to Cuba, he had every right to do so by international law, just as the United States had had the right to place its missiles in Turkey, Italy, and elsewhere, as long as the host government approved. Then there is the question of "offensive" weapons. Kennedy could be justified in taking a hard line against Khrushchev only if the missiles were offensive; he could hardly complain about defensive missiles. Thus, when he made his startling radio-TV address on October 22, he characterized the missiles as offensive. But this is a matter of semantics. To the Americans, their missiles in Turkey were defensive and the Russian missiles in Cuba were offensive. To the Russians, just the opposite was true, which seems to prove that it is always the other side's weapons that are offensive.

In any case, Kennedy decided on a public ultimatum to Khrushchev, and it came with stunning force on that Monday evening, October 22. It is difficult to recapture its fearful impact. Kennedy said that any missile attack from Cuba would mean nuclear retaliation against Russia; he said Cuba would be blockaded (the term "quarantine" was used because it sounded less warlike) and he told Khrushchev in effect: remove those missiles or else.

For a few anxious days it seemed that the situation might well escalate to nuclear war. Each side publicly attacked the other, and there was no sign that Khrushchev would back down. Finally, toward the end of the week, Khrushchev sent messages by a couple of routes: if he removed the missiles, would Kennedy end the blockade and pledge not to invade Cuba? Kennedy said "yes," but for a day or so it seemed that the arrangement might fall through. Then on Sunday, October 28, as the United States was preparing military action against the missile sites which were still under construction, Khrushchev had Radio Moscow announce that a compromise had been reached. The crisis, which had been at the very brink, swiftly faded. One could almost feel the nationwide relief as the terrible tension drained away.

Most Americans hailed the settlement as a great triumph

for Kennedy; he had forced Khrushchev to back down and remove the missiles. There is another school of thought. While recognizing the recklessness of Khrushchev's move, they would argue that Kennedy took the world to the brink of nuclear war to remove missiles that were not an immediate threat and which could have been just as effectively removed by diplomatic means. They also contend that Khrushchev did not back down, that he removed the missiles only after Kennedy had pledged not to invade Cuba. The safety of Cuba, whatever else Khrushchev might have had in mind, was certainly a major factor in sending the missiles. But whoever bore the major responsibility for the nuclear confrontation, it ended without war and led to the partial nuclear test ban treaty and to a period of improved relations between the United States and the Soviet Union.

Although he continued to push the failing Alliance for Progress and continued his economic and diplomatic offensive against Castro, Kennedy in the few months that were left to him had only one further major involvement with Latin America. But that is best told as part of the spectacular intervention by his successor, Lyndon Baines Johnson.

11
The Recent Past

Just as Cuba loomed out of the past to trouble John Kennedy, so, too, did the Dominican Republic affect Lyndon Johnson. Again, as with Cuba, this American intervention was a legacy of a previous one, some forty years before. The earlier American intervention had ended in 1924, the United States leaving behind the marine-trained Guardina Nacional to maintain law and order. Control of the Guard was soon seized by one of its officers, Rafael Trujillo, who by 1930 had taken control of the entire nation. He kept it, by cruel and bloody repression, until he was assassinated on May 30, 1961, not long after John Kennedy had taken office in the United States. Kennedy quickly sent a study team to Santo Domingo that concluded that anti-Communist liberals were not yet strong enough to govern effectively. So Kennedy decided to support Joaquín Balaguer, Trujillo's puppet President, who had long been a henchman of the dictator. Trujillo's brothers and son appeared on the verge of attempting a military takeover, but Kennedy headed that off by sending eight naval ships with

1,800 men aboard to anchor just offshore at Santo Domingo. This convinced the Dominican military to desert the Trujillos and stick with Balaguer.

In the chaos that followed three decades of one-man rule, Balaguer lost control and fled into exile. Kennedy poured money and men into the Dominican Republic to the extent that the United States once again entirely dominated the country. Although there were few Communists in the country and although the threat to democracy came from the right-wing generals, the Kennedy administration, alarmed by Castro's Cuba, concentrated on anti-Communist activity. Needless to say, the old landowning families and the generals needed little encouragement to profess their staunch anti-Communism and to point with alarm at the "Communist menace."

By the end of 1962 free elections were held. The winner, with 62 per cent of the vote, was Juan Bosch, an anti-Trujillo writer who had been exiled for twenty-four years. He was a progressive and the friend of most Latin American democratic reformers. Almost as soon as he was inaugurated in February of 1963, he came under constant attack from the conservatives and military as pro-Communist. He attempted a reform program but the difficulties were enormous in changing from a one-man state to a democratic government, particularly in so underdeveloped a society. And it is true that Bosch may have been a better writer about politics than a practitioner of them. Also he refused to drive the few Communists into exile, believing it was better to defeat them politically by improving the nation's living standards.

Bosch was opposed not only by the political right but by many of the American officials as well. They were upset that he often did not take their advice and worried that he was not being tough enough, they thought, on the Communists. His days were numbered from the beginning. Plans for a coup began soon after he took office and became common knowledge by the end of the summer of 1963. He appealed to the American ambassador for support from the United States. The ambassador asked for a Navy aircraft carrier to cruise offshore as a symbol of American support. He was turned down. Although Kennedy was willing to send a Navy flotilla to support a long-time Trujillo henchman, he was not willing to take similar action in support of a democratically elected president. Bosch was overthrown by an army coup on September 25.

The junta put into power Donald Reid Cabral, whose government was soon recognized by the administration of Lyndon Johnson shortly after he succeeded the slain John Kennedy. Johnson also appointed as Assistant Secretary of State for Latin American affairs, Thomas Mann, a hardline anti-Communist. Reid Cabral had little success in governing. He was faced not only with the economic and social problems that Bosch had found so difficult, but he was opposed on one side by followers of Bosch and on the other by the military whose power he had tried somewhat to curb. By April 1965 both movements were out to oust Reid Cabral. First the pro-Bosch group, which included a number of younger officers, struck. They proclaimed revolution and seized the government radio station. The American embassy thought that the government had things in hand and cabled Washington that the revolution was fizzling. Reid Cabral gave the rebels until five in the afternoon to surrender or be crushed by government troops. He later extended the ultimatum until six the next morning, April 25.[1]

It was a chaotic day that Saturday, the first day of the revolution. The younger, pro-Bosch officers were calling on their colleagues to join them against the older officers who had gained power under Trujillo. Now the older officers struck against Reid Cabral. They refused his orders to attack the younger officers and demanded he resign. He said he would, and the older officers planned to install a junta that would hold elections later in the year. But the older officers found that they had lost their power over the younger men. They opposed a junta and demanded the immediate restoration of constitutional government under Bosch, who was in exile in nearby Puerto Rico.

The old officers now decided to attack the younger. Airplanes bombed and strafed rebel headquarters. The young officers in turn opened up the government armories and gave weapons to the people, who eagerly grabbed everything from pistols to machine guns. Filling stations gave away gasoline so the people could make Molotov cocktails to throw against the tanks of the older officers. By now the American embassy had concluded that something was up. More important, the U.S. officials concluded that the return of Bosch, the legitimately elected President, would mean a Communist Dominican Republic within six months. It is hard to understand how the embassy reached this conclusion. The embassy staff knew that there were only a few militant Communists and that they were weak and divided. They evidently feared that even a few Communists could dominate the nation.

The embassy sent panicky cables to Washington, urging intervention on the side of the right-wing generals. At first, however, it seemed that the old officers would win without U.S. help. For a time, amidst incredible confusion, a stalemate ex-

isted. Then the battle tilted in favor of the old officers as their
tanks spearheaded an advance from a military base into the
rebel-held Santo Domingo. By Tuesday night the rebel effort
seemed on the verge of collapse and the news was flashed
around the world that the revolution was all but over. But
somehow that night the rebels pulled themselves together and
by Wednesday they were on the offensive. Now it was the old
generals who seemed on the verge of defeat. They appealed to
the U.S. embassy for help. The embassy quickly sent the appeal to Washington with its support. Johnson agreed and went
on nationwide TV that same day to report that 400 marines
had already landed in the Dominican Republic "to give protection to hundreds of Americans who are still in the Dominican Republic. . . ." Although Johnson may very well have
been genuinely concerned about the safety of Americans, it
soon became obvious that that was not his main reason for the
intervention.

In any case, this reason was widely disbelieved, at home and
abroad, and a storm of protest began that lasted for weeks,
protest that in later months was switched to criticism of the es-
calating war in Vietnam. The United States informed the UN
Security Council that it had intervened "to protect American
citizens," and it hastened to get the approval of the Organization of American States. It must be emphasized that the
United States went to the O.A.S. only *after* the intervention
had already begun.

By Thursday, April 29, 1965, marines were pouring ashore.
Although the United States was purportedly neutral, the marines immediately began to aid the besieged old officers, who
were out of food and water. They also interposed themselves
between the rebels and "loyalists." There is little doubt that at

the last moment the U.S. marines deprived the rebels of victory.

The protests in the United States and around the world began to grow, particularly when Johnson, on May 2, gave the real reason for the intervention: because "a band of Communist conspirators" was taking control of what had begun as a "popular democratic revolution." Johnson, like Kennedy, was determined that there not be "another Castro" in Latin America. But the United States was totally unable to document its assertion that Communists were taking control. It also charged the rebels with atrocities, only to have it discovered later that the atrocities were committed by the loyalists. At the United Nations the United States was under heavy criticism, not least of all from the Russians. This provided a nice irony. The United States informed the United Nations that the matter was no affair of the world organization, that it was a matter to be decided entirely within the O.A.S. Three years later at the United Nations when the United States criticized Russia for its occupation of Czechoslovakia, Russia in turn replied that it was no concern of that organization, that it was strictly a matter for the Warsaw Pact. Neither great power wanted the United Nations getting involved in such matters.

More than 20,000 American troops had landed in the Dominican Republic, a clear violation of the nonintervention clauses of a number of international agreements. The United States attempted to reduce criticism by getting the O.A.S. to establish an Inter-American Peace Force to remain in the Dominican Republic until peace was established. The measure passed by only one vote, with a majority of the affirmative votes coming from dictatorial countries. A Brazilian general was put in charge of the force, which had tiny token contingents from a handful of nations. The force was almost entirely composed of Americans. They were theoretically under the command of the Brazilian general, but the American general in charge of the U.S. troops undiplomatically told the press that he took his orders from the United States, not the Organization of American States.

Not until September 1965 was some semblance of order to be restored in the Dominican Republic. By that time hundreds of Dominicans had been killed, the intervention had been criticized all over the world, particularly in Latin America, which had hoped that American adherence to nonintervention treaties had meant the end of U.S. intervention. As American troops later began to pull out, American money again poured in, twice as much per capita as in any other Latin nation.

New elections were held in the Dominican Republic on June 1, 1966. Juan Bosch ran again. His opponent was Joaquín Balaguer, who had American support. Bosch was favored to win—but he didn't. Balaguer got about 56 per cent of the vote. Bosch may have been overconfident; he never left his home during the campaign. If he had been less confident, he might have overcome his fear of assassination and campaigned vigorously. To Latin voters *machismo* (masculinity) is very important and Bosch's refusal to expose himself to the real dangers of campaigning in the Dominican Republic no doubt lost him many votes. Balaguer won re-election in 1970 but has made little progress in overcoming his country's difficult problems. The Dominican Republic is still a violent nation, and no one would dare to say that there will not be another revolution against the elite and the military, who are still so influential.

One other legacy from the past was to worry the United

States in the mid 1960s. This time the scene was Panama, that creation of Teddy Roosevelt's in 1903. Even though the United States in 1939 gave up its right to intervene in the country's domestic affairs, Panama, a chronically underdeveloped country, has been dominated by the Canal Zone. The fact that the United States has sovereign rights over the Zone has long irritated some Panamanians, and this irritation occasionally bursts into demonstrations.

In January 1964 a group of Panamanian young people dashed into the Canal Zone and raised their national flag on a pole next to the American flag. A group of young Americans pulled down the Panamanian flag and a riot erupted. U.S. soldiers intervened and by the time the riots had ended, three of them were dead as were twenty-one Panamanians. Panama took the matter to the United Nations and the Organization of American States, and eventually Panama and the United States agreed to negotiate the status of the Canal Zone. The incident was investigated by the International Commission of Jurists, which concluded that the United States had not violated human rights.

In 1967 the two nations negotiated a series of treaties providing for the United States to relinquish its sovereignty over the Canal Zone to a joint U.S.–Panama authority, to increase the payments to Panama, and to integrate the Zone politically with Panama. The United States was also given an option to build a new canal. It is also considering sites in northern Colombia and in Nicaragua. The treaties had not been ratified at this writing.

Since the Dominican and Panamanian adventures, American attention has been turned away from Latin America. The Alliance for Progress, already stumbling, all but died with

President Kennedy. His successors have been almost wholly preoccupied with the tragic war in Vietnam. Only occasionally does Latin America grab for a moment the headlines that it commanded during the early 1960s. And these headlines are often the result of a political kidnaping or murder here and there. The economies of Latin America are still in the gravest difficulty, with a few exceptions. As in the past, these economies depend on a few raw materials often sold at the mercy of the purchasing industrial nations. Latin statesmen still cry for American assistance, but the United States, beset with turmoil over Vietnam and itself troubled by economic problems, continues to reduce its foreign aid programs.

Just as the United States in recent years has largely ignored Latin America, so, too, are some Latin states turning away from the United States. A number of nations are growing increasingly nationalistic and less eager to follow the U.S. lead in international matters. Some of these same nations, such as Chile and Peru, and Bolivia, are less reluctant to nationalize American-owned properties, and in nations where the United States is actively helping governments keep down militant opposition movements, anti-Americanism is growing.

Although American aid for economic development is shrinking, the Nixon administration at this writing was considering an increase in aid to police forces all over the world, including a number in Latin America. This aid would not be for normal police work but to improve police ability to combat "subversive" movements. In the past ten years, for instance, the United States has helped train 100,000 policemen in Brazil, where, in recent years, there have been widespread, and documented, charges of torture by security police. U.S. aid has also been significant in Guatemala, where political violence takes hundreds of lives each year, and in the Dominican Republic. In these and other nations the United States is bitterly accused by opposition elements of aiding in repression.

In a closely related area, President Nixon in the spring of 1971 waived the ceiling of $75 million annually in arms aid to Latin America. This question was discussed by the *New York Times* in an editorial:

. . . Secretary of State Rogers has defended the President's waiver . . . on the ground that it "diminishes the prospects of any powers unfriendly to the United States advancing their influence and objectives in this hemisphere." But the principal rivals to the United States as arms suppliers to the Latins are Britain, France, West Germany and Italy, all allies of the United States. Their competition may be annoying to American arms manufacturers, but such competition in itself poses no threat to American security interests.

What does threaten the security of all of the hemisphere is an incipient Latin arms race that will divert scarce resources from desperately needed development efforts, strengthen antidemocratic regimes and increase the danger and potential magnitude of local conflicts. The United States may be powerless to prevent this madness, but there is no good reason why the American taxpayers should be asked to help finance it.

Up until this moment we have been looking at the past, at what has happened in the relations between the United States and Latin America. But before closing, we must take a look into the future. Not to predict, for that would be folly, but to examine some of the challenges that must be faced, for there is no way to escape them.

12
The Future

One thing is certain about the future of Latin America. It will be dominated by change, change of such a magnitude that it will shake the entire hemisphere. This is an easy prediction. Latin America already has the highest birth rate in the world, and by the year 2000 its population may soar from 225 million to 600 million. Since the region cannot satisfactorily feed all the people it already has, something is going to have to change. If the rate of food production is not multiplied, people will starve. Or Latin America will have to sharply reduce its birth rate. Yet birth control is contrary to centuries of Roman Catholic tradition and dogma.

Something else is inescapable. Whether the population is somehow stabilized or whether it continues to multiply, the people of Latin America, the exploited masses of Indian, African, or mixed parentage, will not be content to remain at their present subsistence standard of living. If in nothing else, America has triumphed in spreading the word that a good life is possible. However they have learned it, through radio or television or movies or newspapers and magazines or word of mouth, these millions of Latin Americans have learned that there is more to life than scraping a bare existence from the fields or mines. They are going to demand a share of this better life from their rulers, and if they do not get it, they will struggle to take it. This has already begun all through Latin America, as all through the world, and there is no way to stop this demand, short of satisfying it. Repression may work for years or even for decades, but it cannot work forever. The elite must share with their countrymen. If they don't do it willingly, they will be forced to do it.

Unfortunately, the elites of the world seldom learn from history. Often they attempt to hold on, not only through selfishness but because they have convinced themselves that civilization will collapse if they don't hold on. The enlightened ones who recognize that they can no longer monopolize their nation's riches must also recognize that their wealth, no matter how vast, will not be enough to satisfy the legitimate aspirations of their countrymen. The nation must generate many more times that wealth, something possible only with economic development far beyond what most of them have dreamed. The various nations will have to mobilize themselves, discipline themselves beyond the demands of past generations, for they will be attempting to do in decades what the industrial nations did in centuries.

As the largest purchaser of Latin raw materials, as its largest supplier of finished goods, as the political leader of the hemisphere, or even as a neighbor in an interdependent world, the United States cannot escape involvement. We have already seen how changes have complicated U.S.–Latin relations. But the changes of the past will be nothing compared to the changes of the future. In the past the military have stood for stability, the status quo. But in a few cases the military themselves have begun to initiate change. For centuries the Church was the very bastion of conservatism, but now in many Latin nations it is young Catholic priests, and some not so young, who are in the forefront of those demanding change. Economic relationships are going to have to shift. Latin America will refuse to be relegated to supplier of raw materials (at low prices) and purchaser of finished goods (at high prices). Gradually, the Latin states will refuse to be automatic followers of the United States in the O.A.S. and the UN.

As things change in Latin America, the United States will have to constantly re-examine its policy. Will it be flexible and change, too, or will it attempt to preserve the old order? Will it encourage change in the authoritarian nations or will it help the dictators to try to stay in power, thus incurring the lasting enmity of those seeking reform? Will it encourage change by concentrating its aid on those governments that promote change and giving minimal assistance to the dictators and the military juntas? Will it stop forever its long practice of intervention? Will it treat its fellow members of the O.A.S. as equals and not as subordinates? Will it recognize that democracy can take many shapes, that Latin traditions and history mandate forms of government different than the American? Will it recognize in short that its days of domination are fast approaching an end?

Perhaps the greatest challenge to U.S. wisdom will be in the economic field. Although American direct interventions have been concentrated in those areas closest to the United States— Mexico, the Caribbean, and Central America—American political influence has been enormous throughout the entire

area, not least because of the huge investments of private corporations and the huge purchases of Latin products: tin and
other minerals in Bolivia; copper and nitrates in Chile; coffee
in Brazil, Colombia, and other countries; lead and other minerals in Peru; petroleum in Venezuela; etc. It is no overstate-
ment to say that American corporations dominate the Latin
American economy. It is commonplace for American officials,
public and private, to speak of the great benefits of American
government loans and grants and of American private investments. Yet the fact is that American business takes more out of
Latin America in profits than it puts in in loans, grants, and
investments. From 1960 through 1967, the early years of the
Alliance for Progress and the United Nation's Development
Decade, the United States put about $1.7 billion into Latin
America and took out about $8.8 billion, a net gain of about
$7.1 billion.

As Latin nations become more nationalistic—and the trend
is already clearly underway—they will obviously try to redress
that imbalance. They can, among other things, nationalize
American firms or put limits on the amount of profit American firms can take out of the country. Nationalization has already begun, and there are usually vast differences between
what the host country thinks is a fair price and what the
American firm believes is fair. Often these questions will be re-
solved by amicable but tough negotiations. Other times the
host country will set a price and say take it or leave it. In extreme cases the host country might argue that the firm has already made such enormous profits that it deserves no further
compensation. Almost without exception, in difficult cases, the
American firm will turn to Washington for assistance. This is a
delicate matter. The United States will want to serve the inter-

ests of the American firm without alienating the host country. Wisdom, moderation, and tact will be required, particularly when the United States feels, as it certainly will on occasion, that the position taken by the host country is wholly indefensible. This will be a particular difficulty in dealing with a nation like Chile, which, in 1970, elected a socialist government, one which the United States almost instinctively suspects, and one which in turn regards the United States with great suspicion. Indeed, severe tensions have already developed over the nationalization of American-owned mining properties.

It would be glib to suggest that it will be simple for any American president to encourage change, foster democracy, and remain calmly tolerant in a period when chaos is more likely than stability. It is easy to say that America should encourage change and democracy, but exactly how does one go about it in a country, say, like Brazil? With its population of some 80 million, with its great riches, actual and potential, with its enormous area, with its importance as a trading partner, with the government's presumably firm control of the nation, exactly how does the United States convince Brazil that it should end its policy of repression? Exactly how does the United States deal with Chile, the first freely-elected Marxist state in the world? How does the United States influence Guatemala to end the bloodletting that has brought terror to the entire spectrum of that poor country's political life? How does the United States deal with the right-wing military in one country and the left-wing military in another? How does the United States remain calm in the face of the provocations, the outrage, even the insults that are bound to occur in the turbulent decades ahead? How does any American president convince his own people, in a time of terrible economic, social, and political problems at home, that they have an obligation to help their southern neighbors? How does an American president, even if his concern is genuine, convince Latin leaders that he has departed from the "big stick" policies of more than a century?

No, it is not going to be easy for any American president to formulate a policy responsive to a period of chaotic change and flexible enough to deal individually with the circumstances of a score of nations, so much alike but each so proud and jealous and sensitive of its individuality. It is not going to be easy but it is going to be necessary. We cannot ignore Latin America because it should not and would not be ignored. Nor, as we have learned in the last decade, can we, despite our enormous strength, force other nations to our will. Somewhere between isolation and intervention we will have to establish a Latin American policy responsive to the needs of all the peoples involved. One place to begin could be with an honest look at the past, from Latin America's point of view as well as our own.

Notes

CHAPTER 1   THE BEGINNING

1. George Pendle, *A History of Latin America,* p. 12. (For complete information on all books referred to in these notes, see the Bibliography.)
2. William H. Prescott's *Conquest of Mexico* and *Conquest of Peru* are classics.
3. Pendle, p. 40.

CHAPTER 2   SPAIN'S GRIP WEAKENS

1. Samuel Flagg Bemis' *The Latin American Policy of the United States* was essential to the preparation of this book. Although Bemis sometimes comes very close to chauvinism, his command of the subject is extraordinary.
2. Pendle, p. 109.
3. Pendle, p. 123.
4. Bemis, p. 44.
5. Frank Tannenbaum, *Ten Keys to Latin America,* pp. 146, 149.
6. Tannenbaum, p. 138.

CHAPTER 3   THE MONROE DOCTRINE

1. Alonso Aguilar, *Pan-Americanism from Monroe to the Present: A View from the Other Side,* p. 43.
2. Aguilar, p. 23.
3. Bemis, p. 56.

4. The entire text of the Monroe Doctrine can be found in my *Beyond Diplomacy*, pp. 221–224.

5. Bemis, p. 70.

6. Bemis, p. 71.

7. American Assembly, *The United States and Latin America*, p. 123.

8. Bemis, p. 98.

9. Bernard DeVoto, *The Year of Decision: 1846*, p. 13.

10. Bemis, p. 99.

11. A brief but detailed account of the Mexican War is given in *Beyond Diplomacy*, pp. 134–139.

12. A complete text of Polk's war message can be found in *Beyond Diplomacy*, pp. 225–228.

13. Bemis, p. 106.

14. Bemis, p. 107.

15. Bemis, p. 107.

16. Bemis, p. 110.

CHAPTER 4   ASSERTING THE DOCTRINE

1. Bemis, p. 112.

2. Bemis, p. 116.

3. Bemis, p. 119.

4. Bemis, p. 120.

5. American Assembly, p. 124.

6. Aguilar, p. 57.

7. Bemis, p. 122.

CHAPTER 5   THE DAWN OF IMPERIALISM

1. Cited in Aguilar, p. 41.

2. H. Wayne Morgan, *America's Road to Empire: The War with Spain and Overseas Expansion*, p. 7.

3. A more complete account of the Spanish–American War than is suitable here can be found in *Beyond Diplomacy*, pp. 53–92.

4. *Beyond Diplomacy*, p. 65.

5. Frank Freidel, *The Splendid Little War*, p. 173.

6. Bemis, p. 144.

7. Aguilar, p. 45.

8. For the complete text, see *Beyond Diplomacy*, pp. 238–239.

CHAPTER 6   DOLLAR DIPLOMACY

1. *Beyond Diplomacy,* p. 97. In this book I discuss Dollar Diplomacy and its incredibly tangled context in much greater detail than is possible here.
2. Tannenbaum, p. 142.
3. Bemis, p. 147.
4. Bemis, p. 149.
5. *Roosevelt Letters,* Roosevelt Papers, Library of Congress, Vol. VI, p. 1491.
6. *Roosevelt Letters,* Vol. IV, p. 801.
7. Dana G. Munro, *Intervention and Dollar Diplomacy in the Caribbean 1900–1921,* p. 13. This is the standard work on the subject.
8. As cited in *Beyond Diplomacy,* p. 113.
9. Munro, p. 216.

CHAPTER 7   PRESIDENT WILSON INTERVENES

1. Bemis, p. 173.
2. Bemis, p. 183.
3. As cited by Aguilar, p. 57.
4. As cited by Aguilar, p. 58.
5. As cited by Aguilar, p. 64.
6. Bemis, p. 246.
7. Bemis, p. 221.
8. Bemis, p. 222.
9. Bemis, p. 222.

CHAPTER 8   THE YEARS OF THE GOOD NEIGHBOR

1. American Assembly, p. 136.
2. *Current History,* June 1969, p. 370.
3. Aguilar, p. 69.
4. Hugh Thomas, *Cuba: The Pursuit of Freedom,* p. 639.
5. Bemis, p. 287.
6. For the complete text of Articles I and II, see *Beyond Diplomacy,* p. 262.
7. Bemis, p. 360.
8. Bemis, p. 368.
9. Bemis, p. 369.

CHAPTER 9   LATIN AMERICA AND THE COLD WAR

1. I discuss this era in detail in my *America and the Cold War*.
2. American Assembly, p. 136.
3. *Washington Post*, December 29, 1948.
4. Richard J. Barnet, *Intervention and Revolution*, p. 229. This book includes a good brief account.
5. As cited by Barnet, p. 231.
6. Barnet, p. 232.
7. American Assembly, p. 143.
8. As cited by Aguilar, p. 101.

CHAPTER 10   THE UNITED STATES *vs.* CUBA

1. As cited by Thomas, p. 128. This book is particularly good on U.S.–Cuban relations of this period.
2. It is covered in detail in a number of books, among them my *Cold War and Counterrevolution: The Foreign Policy of John F. Kennedy.*
3. *Public Papers of the Presidents: John F. Kennedy 1961*. Washington: U.S. Government Printing Office, 1962, p. 304.
4. This is reported by Kennedy's sympathetic biographer, Arthur Schlesinger, on p. 783 of his *A Thousand Days.*
5. These tense days have been fully and fascinatingly discussed in many books. I have treated the crisis in great detail in *Cold War and Counterrevolution: The Foreign Policy of John F. Kennedy*, dissenting from the customary view that Kennedy achieved a great triumph.

· CHAPTER 11   THE RECENT PAST

1. There are a number of accounts of this American intervention, most notably Tad Szulc's *Dominican Diary*. I give a detailed but fairly brief account in *Beyond Diplomacy*.

Bibliography

Starred titles are especially recommended for young adult readers.

THE CARIBBEAN

Draper, Theodore, *Castro's Revolution: Myths and Realities.* New York: Frederick A. Praeger, Inc. (paper)

Freidel, Frank, *The Splendid Little War.* Boston: Little, Brown and Company, 1958.

Martin, John Bartlow, *Overtaken by Events.* Garden City, N.Y.: Doubleday & Company, Inc., 1966.

Matthews, Herbert L., *Fidel Castro.* New York: Simon & Schuster, Inc., 1970.

Perkins, Dexter, *The United States and the Caribbean.* Cambridge, Mass.: Harvard University Press, 1966.

Ruiz, Ramon Eduardo, *Cuba: The Making of a Revolution.* Northampton, Mass.: University of Massachusetts Press, 1968.

Szulc, Tad, *Dominican Diary.* New York: The Delacorte Press, 1966.

Thomas, Hugh, *Cuba: The Pursuit of Freedom.* New York: Harper & Row, Publishers, 1971.

*Williams, Byron, *Cuba: The Continuing Revolution.* New York: Parents Magazine Press, 1969.

167

LATIN AMERICA

Alexander, Robert J., *Today's Latin America*. Garden City, N.Y.: Doubleday & Company, Inc., Anchor Books, 1968. (paper)

*Baker, Nina B., *He Wouldn't Be King: The Story of Simón Bolívar*. New York: Vanguard Press, Inc., 1941.

Belaunde, Victor A., *Bolívar and the Political Thought of the Spanish–American Revolution*. New York: Octagon Books, 1967.

Council on Foreign Relations, *Social Change in Latin America Today*. New York: Vintage Books, 1961. (paper)

*Gerassi, John, *The Great Fear in Latin America*. New York: P. F. Collier, Inc., 1965.

Herring, Hubert, *A History of Latin America*. New York: Alfred A. Knopf, Inc., 1961.

Horowitz, Irving Louis, Castro, Josué de, and Gerassi, John, *Latin American Radicalism*. New York: Vintage Books, 1969. (paper)

MacEoin, Gary, *Revolution Next Door: Latin America in the 1970s*. New York: Holt, Rinehart & Winston, Inc., 1971.

*Pendle, George, *A History of Latin America*. Baltimore: Penguin Books, 1969. (paper)

Petras, James, and Zeitlin, Maurice, *Latin America: Reform or Revolution?* New York: Fawcett, 1968. (paper)

Schurz, William, *Latin America*. New York: E. P. Dutton & Co., Inc., 1964. (paper)

Szulc, Tad, *Latin America*. New York: Atheneum Publishers, 1967. (paper)

Tannenbaum, Frank, *Ten Keys to Latin America*. New York: Vintage Books, 1966. (paper)

Tomasek, Robert D., ed., *Latin American Politics: Studies of the Contemporary Scene*. Garden City, N.Y.: Anchor Books, 1970. (paper)

Whittaker, Arthur P., *The United States and the Independence of Latin America, 1800–1830*. New York: W. W. Norton & Company, Inc., 1964. (paper)

MEXICO

*Baker, Nina B., *Juarez, Hero of Mexico.* New York: McGraw-Hill Book Company, 1951. (paper)

DeVoto, Bernard, *The Year of Decision: 1846.* Boston: Houghton Mifflin Company, Sentry Edition, 1961. (paper)

*Prescott, William H., *Conquest of Mexico.* New York: Washington Square Press. (paper)

Simpson, L. B., *Many Mexicos.* Berkeley, Cal.: University of California Press. (paper)

Tannenbaum, Frank, *Mexico: The Struggle for Peace and Bread.* New York: Alfred A. Knopf, Inc., 1950.

U.S.–LATIN AMERICAN RELATIONS

Aguilar, Alonso, *Pan-Americanism from Monroe to the Present: A View from the Other Side.* New York: Monthly Review Press, 1968. (paper)

American Assembly, *The United States and Latin America,* Herbert L. Matthews, ed., New York: Spectrum Books, 1963. (paper)

Barnet, Richard J., *Intervention and Revolution.* New York: World Publishing Co., 1968.

Bemis, Samuel Flagg, *The Latin American Policy of the United States.* New York: W. W. Norton & Company, 1967. (paper)

Dulles, Foster Rhea, *The Imperial Years.* New York: Thomas Y. Crowell Company, Apollo Edition, 1956.

Levinson, Jerome, and DeOnis, Juan, *The Alliance That Lost Its Way.* Chicago: Quandrangle Books, Inc., 1970.

Morgan, H. Wayne, *America's Road to Empire: The War with Spain and Overseas Expansion.* New York: John Wiley & Sons, Inc., 1965. (paper)

Munro, Dana G., *Intervention and Dollar Diplomacy in the Caribbean 1900–1921.* Princeton, N.J.: Princeton University Press, 1964.

Radosh, Ronald, *American Labor and United States Foreign Policy*. New York: Random House, Inc., 1969.

Schlesinger, Arthur, *A Thousand Days*. Boston: Houghton Mifflin Company, 1965.

*Walton, Richard J., *America and the Cold War*. New York: The Seabury Press, Inc., 1969.

*————, *Beyond Diplomacy*. New York: Parents Magazine Press, 1970.

————, *Cold War and Counterrevolution: The Foreign Policy of John F. Kennedy*. New York: The Viking Press, Inc., 1972.

————, *The Remnants of Power: The Tragic Last Years of Adlai Stevenson*. New York: Coward-McCann, Inc., 1968.

Index